William Nast

William Nast

patriarch of german methodism

by CARL WITTKE

wayne state university press detroit 1959

copyright © 1960

wayne state university press, detroit 2

all rights reserved

library of congress catalog card number 60–5382

PREFACE

This volume is intended not only to provide a short biography of a unique figure in American church history, but also to add another chapter, albeit a minor one, to the history of German immigration to the United States, and more specifically, to give the story of an immigrant church.

William Nast, patriarch of German Methodism in America, made significant contributions to his church and his times as an author, preacher, theologian and editor; but he was almost equally concerned with the problem of making his fellow German immigrants into good American citizens, and he believed that a German-speaking church, based on the Methodist way of life, would not only save souls but also produce good Americans.

The principal source for this study is the papers of William Nast which his granddaughter, Dr. Marie Nast Wherry of Cincinnati, made available to me, without restrictions of any kind. Another important source is *Der Christliche Apologete*, the Cincinnati German Methodist journal which Nast edited for half a century. Mr. Clyde L. Haselden, Librarian of Baldwin-Wallace College, generously made an almost complete file of the *Apologete* available to me under the most favorable circumstances. Because so much of the narrative is based on the Nast papers and the journal which he edited, I have reduced the number of footnotes to a minimum.

C. W.

CONTENTS

vii

WILLIAM NAST *patriarch of german methodism*

1

SWABIA'S SON

William Nast, known in American church history as the father of German Methodism, was descended from a long line of sturdy Swabian ancestors who for several centuries had provided the Lutheran church of Württemberg with clergymen, the schools with teachers, and the state with minor public officials. Although the Nast family tree may be traced back well into the fifteenth century, we may begin with Johann David Nast who came from Bavaria to Herrenberg in Württemberg in the first half of the seventeenth century and became the town's official musician. From church records, kept so meticulously in the parishes of Germany, we learn that he was a cornetist and bugler, that he was twice married and the father of five children, and that he died in Herrenberg in 1694. His eldest son (1657-1740) became the village musician for Schondorf, and like his father before

3

him, was charged with playing a Lutheran chorale each noonday from the gallery of the local church tower. A younger brother was an oboist and a castle guard at Herrenberg.

One of Johann David Nast's grandsons was the village musician for Leunberg; another was trained as a forester. A great-great-grandson, also named Johann, was preceptor in the Karlsschule in Stuttgart, a teacher in the Obergymnasium, and finally, pastor in Plöchingen, where he died in 1822. His career as minister, pedagog and author of a book on the language of Homer was sufficiently important to assure him a place in Germany's national dictionary of biography.[1] A younger brother became Wilhelm Nast's father.

The Nast genealogy is long and involved and need not be followed in greater detail here. The fact that one of the Nasts had twelve sons and one of these likewise had twelve sons does not make the task of the genealogist any less complicated. A number of the Nasts were active in small businesses or worked for the government in various minor posts. All apparently had benefitted from a thorough elementary education; a number finished the Gymnasium; and several studied philosophy and theology at the University of Tübingen.

The father of Wilhelm Nast, Johann Wilhelm Nast, was thirty-three years old in 1788, when he married Elizabethe Magdalene Ludovika Böhm, a young lady some years her husband's junior, and the descendant of a family which had lived from 1686 to 1759 in a patrician house, built in 1614, on the market place of Stuttgart. Fräulein Böhm's great-grandfather had been a merchant and court official in Stuttgart; her grandfather was also active in business and government service, and her father was a military man, who at one time saw service in the Austrian army.

Of the married life of Johann Nast and Elizabethe Böhm

we know little, and it came to an end with her death in 1824. Ten children were born of their union, of whom five died in early childhood. Among the five who grew to adulthood, the oldest, born in 1789, was named Elizabethe Friedericke Wilhelmine Franziska. She married a theologian, Dr. Süsskind of Stuttgart, who occupied an influential position in the Lutheran state church of Württemberg and had considerable influence on the career of his wife's younger brother. The second of Wilhelm Nast's sisters, Henriette Friedericke Ludovika, died in 1862 at the age of seventy-two. A third sister, Henriette Louise (1795-1865) married Gottlieb Christian Kern, a professor in the Lower Seminary in Schonthal, and later, the pastor of the church in Dürrmenz-Mühlacker. Their daughter married Johann Gottlob Pfleiderer, who became a teacher in Kornthal. Friedrich Wilhelm Nast, the only brother of Wilhelm, was a customs official in Reutlingen.

Wilhelm, the youngest of the family, was born in Stuttgart January 15, 1807, and baptized into the Lutheran church five days later as Johann Wilhelm Nast. The boy lost his father when he was fourteen, and his mother died when he was seventeen. An orphan at seventeen, he became the responsibility of the Süsskinds, his eldest sister and her husband. He attended school in Stuttgart and in Baihingen-an-der-Enz, and evidently made satisfactory progress in his studies. The loss of both parents, and his constant exposure to a theological environment in the home of his brother-in-law, where it was assumed that he would grow up to be a minister of the gospel, may have greatly affected his emotional stability during his adolescent years and may help to account for some of his later religious experiences.

After two years of catechetical instruction by his brother-in-law, Nast at fourteen was pronounced ready for confirmation—an experience which he seems to have anticipated with unusual seriousness. According to accounts of his early life, written many years later for his German Methodist followers in the United States, who were eager for every detail about their leader's religious experiences, young Nast secretly attended conventicles and prayer meetings of German Pietists in his neighborhood and read a number of their religious tracts. For several weeks before his confirmation, he apparently suffered from a deep conviction of sin. On the night of his confirmation, he reported many years later, his heart was "oppressed with sin and guilt," as he wandered out alone, into a rainy night, "to commune with God." "The next morning the whole creation appeared to me as it had never done before. On every blade of grass I saw the imprint of the goodness of God. . . . My heart had peace with God and love to all men." The young confirmant was certain that the Lord had heard his anguished cries, and that his petition to Jesus to save his soul and give him "a new heart" had been granted.

Then he decided to prepare for missionary work in heathen lands and talked of going to a mission institute to get the necessary training, but his relatives, including his mother, decided otherwise. They were convinced that the boy was destined for a more formal career in theology, as a member of the established Lutheran church, and that he would follow in the footsteps of a number of his forebears who had been Lutheran ministers for generations. So, at fourteen, he was enrolled in the Lower Seminary at Blaubeuren, to prepare himself for further study at the University of Tübingen.[2]

Blaubeuren is a charming little town in Württemberg, surrounded by hills and high, rugged rock formations, a short distance from Ulm, and still an attraction for tourists because of its famous *Blautopf* (Blue Bowl), a clear blue pool of water, some sixty-five feet deep, situated just above the town. Blaubeuren had been the seat of an old Benedictine abbey, and, after the Reformation, its Gothic cloister had been converted into a Protestant seminary. The cloister, lying in a lovely valley, with the little town hugged closely around it, has stalls, carved in 1493, a high altar with life-like figures of Mary and her baby Jesus, and paintings of the early Swabian school which depict the history of John the Baptist. In this romantic, historic place, young Nast spent the next four years.

He was one of about fifty boys in his class in the Lower Seminary in Blaubeuren, one of four schools maintained by Württemberg to prepare young men for the Protestant ministry. Among his classmates were Wilhelm Waillinger, the Swabian poet; Eduard Mörike, who became a writer and lyric poet of distinction; [3] Wilhelm Hoffmann, a prominent court preacher in later years; Carl Fischer, who became a professor of aesthetics and to whom Nast often referred as "the dearest friend of my youth"; several future revolutionists of the German uprisings of 1848-49; and David Friedrich Strauss, whose *magnum opus, The Life of Jesus*, was published in 1835, in the same year that Nast began his religious mission to the Germans of Cincinnati. In this book, and in sharp contrast with the theology of his former classmate, Strauss tried to reconcile science, philosophy and religion and to combine Hegelianism and Christianity. The book precipitated a violent intellectual revolution in German theological circles, and the author became a stormy, controversial figure throughout Western Europe. [4]

Nast was a conscientious, satisfactory student at Blaubeuren, but he would hardly have been singled out among such a galaxy of promising classmates as intellectually unusual. He acquired a thorough training in the ancient languages, Greek, Latin and Hebrew. He read Moses and the prophets in Hebrew and the New Testament in Greek. His Greek teacher was Ferdinand Christian Baur, soon to move to a professorship in Tübingen. The curriculum also included logic, history and several other subjects. The small faculty were thorough classical scholars, admirers of antiquity, and rationalists. Their students read the books of the Bible as an exercise in literary criticism, rather than as a source of divine revelation. In Nast's own words, they "stripped the Hebrew Old Testament Scriptures of all their Messianic truth," and fed their students on "the nectar and ambrosia of classical paganism."

Nast's inner struggle for salvation and peace caused him many hours of mental anguish as he labored over his studies at Blaubeuren. He read Arndt's *Wahres Christentum* and Thomas à Kempis and other mystics. He was shocked to find clergymen patronizing the taverns and people playing cards on Sunday. After his first year, however, he too yielded to the worldly attractions of student life, and apparently became less concerned about the morals of some of his fellow students whose quest for pleasure could hardly have been very harmful. The sole object of his classmates, he wrote years later, "was not to become ambassadors for Christ, but heroes, poets and philosophers. Only one inquired after the Saviour of sinners."

Whatever his problems and anxieties, as he continued to wrestle with unsolved religious questions, he received an excellent education in the fundamentals at Blaubeuren, according to the exacting standards and discipline of the German Gymnasium. What he learned at Blaubeuren and later in Tübingen stood him in good stead later and made

him a unique figure among his early Methodist colleagues in
the United States, most of whom had very little book learning.
At eighteen he passed the necessary qualifying examinations
for admission to the University of Tübingen, and the state
of Württemberg continued to subsidize his education as a
prospective minister of the established church.

Strauss went with him to Tübingen, and there both
re-encountered Ferdinand Baur, now a member of the faculty.
Both Strauss and Baur had a profound influence on Nast,
although he finally revolted completely against their rationalist
philosophy and sought salvation from an entirely different
source. Yet he always testified to the fine, moral character of
David Strauss and to his politeness and affability and sincerity,
though he found him somewhat opinionated, cold-blooded
and too much interested in the abnormal. Strauss felt at
home at Tübingen and became absorbed in Baur's lectures
and in the philosophy of Hegel and Schleiermacher, which
he emphasized. Nast, on the other hand, was profoundly
disturbed by many of the things he heard in the lecture hall,
but he continued his friendly relations with his fellow students
and met regularly with them and other members of a club
to which they belonged in a tavern where the young men
could carry on their disputations over a glass of beer.

Strauss, in his *Das Leben Jesu, kritisch bearbeitet* (The
Life of Jesus, Critically Considered), which he published
eight years after he and Nast were fellow students in
Tübingen, contended that the Gospels represented primarily
the myths of the early Christian communities rather than
historical fact. He became a humanist and a pantheist, and
stressed the divinity of humanity, rather than one God turned
man in the person of Jesus. He won and lost a teaching post
in Tübingen, and then was prevented from accepting an

appointment as professor at Zürich. Nast found the liberal, rationalist atmosphere of the University of Tübingen more and more uncongenial and unsettling. He thought he had had some experience with "experimental religion," and he did not take kindly to the lectures of Baur who taught the "mystical theory of the gospels" and during his many years at Tübingen developed the "Tübinger School" which pioneered in scientific research in the field of early Christianity. Nevertheless, when Baur died in 1861, Nast devoted an article in *Der Christliche Apologete*, of which he had been the editor for a number of years, to his former teacher. The piece was entitled "The Death of a Pantheist," and paid a warm tribute to Baur's great learning, his eloquence and personal attractiveness. Nast called him the Voltaire of his age.[5]

Nast remained at Tübingen for two years, until he was twenty. He was drawn, to quote his own words, "into the mists of German Transcendentalism and dreamy speculations," and became "lost in the labyrinth of Pantheism." He found himself "divorced from the evangelical faith," "without a rudder or compass, without God and without hope, under the dominion of sin and Satan." When he reached a point in his confused thinking which led him to reject the Lutheran articles of religion because of the rationalist views he had absorbed from his Tübingen professors, he decided that the time had come to abandon his theological studies. The decision required him to pay back the financial assistance he had received from the state, but with the help of his relatives he met his obligations in full.

Nast returned to his native Stuttgart in "a whirl of doubt." He received some help during this period of intellectual and emotional upheaval by attending the services of Ludwig Hofacker, a devout preacher who pleaded with sinners to repent and come to the mercy seat. Nast also found a measure of peace and security in the family circle of his married sisters. But he could not be idle long, and so resolved to study art and prepare himself for a career in belles lettres. After spending some time in Vienna, Munich and Dresden, he discovered that he had no special talents for an artistic career and that his excursions into art and literature did not give him the peace of mind he craved. In Weinsberg he visited the poet Justinus Kerner, and in Dresden he went to see Ludwig Tieck, philosopher and "father of the romantic school," whom he admired. Tieck urged him to give up aesthetics and return to his studies in Tübingen, and gave him a letter to Dr. Süsskind, Nast's brother-in-law, urging the latter to use his influential position in the church to help the young man gain readmission to the university.

Meantime, it may be assumed, Nast had learned something about America, to which so many of his fellow Germans were going. He could not help being impressed by the tales about this new land of liberty which circulated in Germany, thanks largely to "America letters" from venturesome emigrants who sent home good reports of what they found in the United States. Nast learned that there were few teachers of the classics in America and concluded that his chances to get a teaching post were good. Süsskind urged his young brother-in-law to make a new beginning in the United States, and probably was somewhat relieved when he left for America. According to one account, Nast also had consulted a well-known clairvoyant who reassured him that he would find both success and peace in a distant land. In any event, on September 28, 1828, at the age of twenty-one, he landed in New York, eager to begin a new career.

2

A ROMANTIC INTERLUDE

pon his arrival in New York, Nast called on several Lutheran clergymen, who received him indifferently. For a short time he found employment as a tutor in Millersburg, Pennsylvania, and then moved on to Duncan's Island (also in Pennsylvania) to tutor the two boys of the widow Rebecca Duncan. Mrs. Duncan owned considerable property, and Nast received board and lodging, and thirty dollars a month. Here too began what was probably the most romantic and certainly one of the most disturbing episodes in his lifetime.

In a letter of June 8, 1830, to relatives in Germany, Nast explained that he received the appointment as tutor on Duncan's Island through the good offices of a senator whom he had met quite by accident; that his original intention had been to read medicine, while he made his living as a private teacher; and that he found it "hard to leave" the island, because of the many kindnesses of his employer, who had made him feel immediately at home in a strange country, had "fitted him out" like a member of the family, and had treated him like a brother.

This letter was a model of understatement, as far as his relations with the widow Duncan were concerned, for despite a difference of some eighteen years in their ages, all the evidence points to the fact that the two became involved in a romance from which it took years to extricate themselves and which left a deep impression on their lives. Historians of German Methodism have ignored the episode, or merely have reported Nast's stay on Duncan's Island without reference to the emotional crisis which it precipitated. Modern Freudians undoubtedly would relate the several periods of doubt and acute depression which Nast suffered in later years to the experiences and repressions of this earlier day. What was really involved in this romance cannot be clearly established. Propinquity undoubtedly led to a period of lovemaking, and there were serious discussions of a possible marriage. It may be that the romance never progressed beyond lovers' caresses, for when Nast refers in his letters to Rebecca to "carnal" love he may have meant nothing more than to express his conviction that "earthly affection" was not sufficient, that there must be the strongest religious affinity between man and wife, and that, according to the apostolic rule, a man and woman must "marry only in the Lord." It is significant that Nast preserved the letters and the diary to which he confided his experiences with Rebecca. He might well have destroyed them in later life, and thus wiped out all further reference to his sojourn on Duncan's Island, but evidently he believed that there was nothing so unworthy in the

episode which occurred in his early manhood that it constituted a serious reflection upon either his future career as a
minister of the gospel or upon the character of the object
of his affections.

This romantic interlude in his career, as he was slowly
and painfully groping his way toward the acceptance of the
Methodist faith, is worth following in some detail, not only
because it is a fragment of human history from the lives of
two honest and tortured souls, but because it undoubtedly had
great effect upon Nast's struggle for peace and serenity and
salvation, which was particularly acute in his unsettled mind
during his first years in the United States.

Duncan's Island lies at the mouth of the Juniata River,
about fourteen miles above Harrisburg. One of its earliest
settlers was Marcus Hulings, who died in 1788 and who lies
buried on the little island alongside his wife, who had died
before the Revolution. Of the five sons who survived, Thomas
Hulings was the youngest. He was born in 1755, succeeded
to the parental estate, and died in 1808. He was a prominent
man in this part of Pennsylvania and married the daughter
of General Frederick Watts, of the Continental Army. One
of the children of this union, Rebecca Hulings, born March
25, 1789, in 1811 married Robert Callender Duncan, son of
Judge Duncan of Carlisle, from whom Duncan's Island derived its name. Rebecca Duncan had two children: Thomas,
who became a doctor, died without issue, and Benjamin
Styles Duncan, who died in 1870, leaving four children
residing on the island. During the first decade of the nineteenth century, the island was named Isle Benvenue, for in
Rebecca Duncan's will (she died in 1850) she referred to her
residence as Isle Benvenue.[1]

Nast took up residence with the widow and her two boys

in a spacious and impressive home, for Rebecca was a lady of some means. For nearly two years, this little group was together on the little island—it was about two miles long and had only a tiny village and post office at its eastern end. Itinerant Methodist preachers from the Baltimore Conference occasionally stopped to preach and pray at the Duncan home, but one can well imagine that other visitors were few.

After Nast left Duncan's Island for West Point, he began a diary to which he confided all his inner struggles, first in German, then in English, for he became completely bilingual in an amazingly short time. From this diary and a number of letters exchanged between him and Rebecca, their story must be reconstructed, although religion and love were so closely interwoven that it becomes difficult to estimate which was the stronger force. Nast's diary begins with the sentence, "God has seized me again," and it is full of abject self-denunciations of its author's "sinful life," which seems to have involved nothing more serious than "Pride, Anger, Lying and Indolence," though Nast also wrote, "I have enjoyed everything that is forbidden." There are entries referring to his ardent prayers for humility and grace; the need to fast, pray and work for salvation, and a decision to give up coffee, meat and tobacco. The physical consequences of "wrestling" with Satan led to an entry indicating that he had to take calomel for his disturbed gall-bladder.

The diary is full of quotations from religious literature, from St. Augustine to Jeremy Taylor on repentance, from German and British philosophers and theologians, and from Latin and Greek sources. One day Nast went to a camp meeting and was deeply moved, only to have "the Evil One" devastate his soul again. He made a trip to New York, spent money "foolishly" and had "the little spark of faith . . .

extinguished" again by "the desires of the flesh." On another occasion he castigated his spirit for letting his barber persuade him to go hiking and skating, diversions which he considered sinful. The diary is full of instances of its author's wrestling for peace of mind; comments on "the doctrine of regeneration" and the depravity of man; doubts as to the welfare of his soul; and accounts of how he intermittently won and lost his faith. It is the story of a tortured soul, crying for deliverance, and it is a vital part of that religious experience which finally led to his conversion as a Methodist.

Inextricably intertwined with the account of his struggle for religion are many references to his relations with Rebecca, whom he had left behind on Duncan's Island. Perhaps the struggle to attain salvation outweighed in importance his affair of the heart, but each affected the other, and both must be kept in mind in order to understand the psychological crisis through which Nast was passing.

Nast continued to correspond with Rebecca Duncan for several years. Some of his letters were entrusted only to his diary and were never mailed. On June 13, 1831, he recorded the receipt of a long-awaited letter, which revealed "the good, simple, sensible but light-hearted woman" who had stirred his affections, but also revealed how little they understood each other. When he replied, he quoted from Taylor about how "the longing after sensual pleasures is the dissolution of the spirit of man and makes it . . . unapt for spiritual employment." Two weeks later, two letters from Rebecca moved him to reaffirm his love "for this loving woman." "I had sweet emotions today in thinking of Rebecca," he wrote, but he also expressed the hope that "she would find the Lord again." When Rebecca was tardy about replying to his letters, Nast manifested deep concern lest he had "destroyed her peace" by too much preaching about religion and salvation. On December 3, 1831, he recorded, "I feel so lost to-day. The tie between me and Rebecca has become so loose again. She seems to be completely absorbed in the worldly."

Nast copied passages about marriage, including the admonition not to "deceive thyself by overexpecting happiness in the married estate," into his diary, yet in the fall of 1832, he wrote to Rebecca that "we could make each other unspeakably happy if the love of God was the ruling principle in our hearts" and begged her to pray for his soul. He apparently was as deeply concerned with making Rebecca "a bride of Christ, a daughter of the Almighty," as with his own soul. But he added immediately that he did not mean to imply that she loved him "from carnal motives." He knew their feelings had "a nobler origin" even when she yielded to "his wild desires." What he meant by such expressions is difficult to determine. He pointed out that "the knowledge of good and evil" had been developed in him "to a degree which a child of nature" like Rebecca could not fully comprehend. He wanted Rebecca "to be renewed" in the sight of the Lord, so that her love for him might be pure in the eyes of God also, and he blamed himself for having led her temporarily away from Him. There were further references to what made a happy "Christian pair," and when Rebecca began to doubt his love, he chided her for mistrusting his feelings, "whilst so many a kiss yet burns on your lips." Nast's struggle with his conscience may perhaps be summarized in a final quotation from the diary. "I loved you more deeply and more faithfully than men commonly do, but I did not love you *sincerely* . . . because I was not a Christian, for only a Christian can love sincerely."

In March 1832, Nast confessed that he was no longer

certain "that our union is pleasing to Providence," but if Rebecca were convinced that it was otherwise, he would go to the altar with her. When he discussed the matter with an American Calvinist, the latter advised strongly against the marriage, and pointed out serious differences between the lovers because of conflicting religious and ethnic backgrounds. Misgivings "about the lawfulness of our love" now appeared in the diary more frequently and, still more often, doubts about whether Nast was spiritually prepared to assume all the responsibilities of manhood. When Rebecca was depressed by such reflections, he became convinced that God was preparing her for Himself, and advised her "to thank Him for her suffering."

Eventually, Rebecca offered to release him from their engagement, so that he might finally decide whether he loved her "from choice." Nast replied that they were "destined for each other," but that "Providence itself has prevented our union this year." By the spring of 1832, Rebecca refused to see him, and thereafter her letters became shorter and fewer. On March 1, 1833, she wrote to him in Gambier, Ohio, where he was teaching at Kenyon College, to express concern over his bitterness and despair. "I believe you were a better and much happyer man last faul," she added, "than you are now. Oh, that I could recall the tranquillity that we then enjoyed." She urged him to come to the island, where, as his best friend, she would strive to make him comfortable and happy. "The house seems barren without you." Perhaps to prod him into action, she added that she was being courted by a doctor, but would marry only for love.

Six months later Rebecca wrote again because she was offended by the "few disconnected lines" Nast had sent her. She urged him to give up his "foolish talk" about his want of religion, and added, " It keeps you unhappy as well as all others who know you. My troubles are ten times greater than yours." She resented that he thought she was the cause of all his sin, deplored the changes that had come over him in three years, but assured him of her everlasting friendship, and enclosed ten dollars in the letter. Nearly two weeks later she wrote again, addressing him as " Dear Brother." In reply to a letter in which he had written that he was without friends and would soon be unemployed, she advised him to get a teaching position in the common schools, but she did not want him back on the island, where there would be nothing for an " unsettled mind " to do. She pointed out that she could not take him into her home, unless they were married, and that this was now impossible, for the past was irretrievably lost. " What your motives were for pretending to love me, I know not "; she added, " your religious sentiments had some bad effects upon me but they have long since gone." She concluded that sympathy for his desolate situation had probably aroused her affections, and " then you professed so much for me that it heightened my flame." She thanked God that they had escaped matrimony, closed with bitter comments about his flatteries, and vowed never to be deceived again.

Nast returned the money Rebecca had sent him to help him meet expenses at Gambier, and Rebecca replied, deeply hurt, addressing him this time as " Dear Sir." The letter reaffirmed the purity of her love and blamed Nast's friends at West Point for corrupting his feelings toward her. It closed with the hope that they might meet in heaven. Six months later, she wrote again to advise him to continue teaching and not to go into business; and in a final letter, April 29, 1834, she advised him to get married. It " would give you confidence in yourself and compel you to industry," she told him. The rest of the letter was devoted to activities on the island, news about her two boys, the servant problem, the visits of itinerant preachers, and best wishes for a happy marriage. In 1880, when the widow of his youthful affections had been in her grave for thirty years, Nast revisited Duncan's Island while on an eastern trip. He was accompanied by a Methodist minister, Daniel Hartmann, whom he had met on the island many years before. In the *Apologete* Nast described his visit with one of Mrs. Duncan's sons and with the widow of the other. He went to Rebecca's grave to pray with the family. His nostalgic account in the *Apologete* ended with the words, "what emotions overpowered me, I cannot begin to put into words. These were solemn moments." [2]

Meantime, much had happened in Nast's restless quest for security, emotional stability, and the peace of mind which he thought he could find only in religion. He had left Duncan's Island for West Point, where he worked as librarian and instructor in German. In a letter to relatives in Stuttgart, more legible than most of his communications in the German script, he told how he went by stagecoach to Harrisburg and Philadelphia, then by steamer to New York, and up the Hudson, which reminded him of the Rhine, although he missed the ruins of medieval castles. He commented on the canals which were linking the East and the West; he described the palisades of the Hudson; recounted bits of Indian lore and wrote about the historic sites of the American Revolution. He also wrote of his work at the military academy and the books he found in its library.

At West Point, he continued to read the leading theologians, and was so impressed by Jeremy Taylor's *Rule of Holy Living* that he tried the life of an ascetic for a short time. He translated a German theological treatise for the *Princeton*

Review. He became acquainted with two young officers who
had been converted by the academy chaplain, and taught
them Hebrew. And he came to know Charles Pettit McIlvaine,
a Princeton graduate and a strong-headed, rugged ecclesiastic,
who preached evangelical theology to the cadets.

Across the Hudson, Nast attended meetings in the
Methodist chapel of Reverend James J. Romer, and he heard
Dr. Wilbur Fisk, first president of Wesleyan College in
Connecticut, preach at West Point, and was so impressed
that he continued to correspond with him. Meantime,
McIlvaine had become the rector of St. Anne's Protestant
Episcopal Church in Brooklyn and invited Nast to open a
classical school there, but an outbreak of cholera kept him
from accepting the call.

Nast did not like " the godless atmosphere of the military
academy," and decided to return to Duncan's Island. En
route, he stopped at Gettysburg, where he was advised to
return to the Lutheran fold and was offered a place on the
faculty of Gettysburg College as a teacher of ancient languages. At Duncan's Island he again encountered Methodist
itinerants at a camp meeting on the shores of the Juniata and
was so moved that he reported that he wept for several days,
" without stopping." When fall came, he found himself so
mentally and emotionally disturbed that he could not begin
teaching at Gettysburg, but he joined a Methodist class instead and wrote to Dr. Fisk about the religious crisis and the
deep melancholy in which he found himself. The latter told
him to reject his sins and turn to Christ, as a duty which
could not be neglected without divine displeasure.

Nast went west to Pittsburgh, where he attended further
camp meetings on the banks of the Monongahela. For a week,
he worked in the fields with fellow Württembergers at

Economy, Pennsylvania, where the followers of Johann Rapp, a mystic and pietist, had established a successful communistic religious community. Rapp set him to work digging potatoes, as therapy for his disturbed soul, but Nast found manual labor without profit and continued to wrestle for salvation in his own way. From Economy, he went to a farm in Gallia County, Ohio, to tutor several children and to regain his health, which had been seriously affected by his enduring penitential struggles. Here he met Adam Miller, a pioneer Methodist preacher, who had great influence on Nast's later career and who set him to work translating the articles and rules of the Methodist Episcopal church into German.

His friend McIlvaine, who had meantime become Episcopal bishop of Ohio, in 1833 became ex officio the president of Kenyon College. It was through McIlvaine's heroic efforts to raise money that the little college was saved several times from financial collapse. McIlvaine was sympathetic toward all forms of evangelical religion and offered Nast a teaching position in 1834.

The Kenyon catalogue for 1834-35 lists a George R. Williams, A. M., as principal of the Senior Preparatory Department of Kenyon College, and William Nast, A. M., as his assistant. Where Nast acquired the degree remains a mystery —it was probably added for purposes of the catalogue, and in view of his excellent training at Tübingen with more justification than in most cases. Nast did not teach in the college, but in the preparatory department, which offered courses in the ancient languages, English grammar, arithmetic and bookkeeping, geography, history, mathematics, "conversations in chemistry and natural philosophy," rhetoric, logic, composition, declamation, map drawing, modern languages and the principles of teaching. How the two-man faculty divided this staggering curricular load we have no way of knowing. There were forty-one students in their care, ranging from fifteen years of age upward, and the total enrollment at Kenyon at the time was 142. The only student in residence who later achieved prominence was Henry Winter Davis, then a freshman, and later a prominent abolitionist.[3] The records do not show Nast's salary, but the faculty scale for full professors was $400, a house, and pasturage for one cow. The person who served in a position somewhat corresponding to dean of the faculty, received $518.35. It is not indicated whether he kept a cow.

We may assume that Nast's salary was considerably below these figures, and we may also assume that he was adequately trained for his teaching duties. Of greater importance is the fact that while at Kenyon, Nast finally achieved the "conversion" for which his soul had yearned for years and which enabled him to find his place in the bosom of Methodism.

3

WESLEYANISM IN ENGLAND AND AMERICA

𝔄merican Methodism was the child of British Wesleyanism. The Methodist movement was born of historical forces in England which arose primarily from the Industrial Revolution, and it had its origin in the character, vision, and persistent efforts of one man, John Wesley, whom Nast admired and with whose career he thought his own had certain parallels.

Methodism was born in a time of sharp class distinctions in English society and amid gross inequities in the social and economic structure of the state, which had been greatly aggravated by the early, unhappy consequences of the Industrial Revolution. The Established Church, to say nothing of other agencies, had paid little attention to the poor who crowded the city slums, to the disinherited peasants who were the victims of a sweeping agricultural revolution, or to the women and children who worked long hours under pitiful conditions in factories and coal pits. It was customary to refer to the common people as "the mob," who had to be held in line by a ferocious criminal code. Far from being deeply concerned over the plight of the underprivileged, too many churchmen held sinecures and completely neglected their charges, and some engaged in a manner of living hardly compatible with the standards of the Man of Galilee.

It was John Wesley's major concern to carry religion to the unchurched and neglected masses and to revive hope in their hearts by preaching about the possibility for every man to establish a personal fellowship with God, whatever his temporal status might be. Instead of the stern Calvinist doctrine of predestination, Wesley preached a message of promise which gave even the most seasoned sinner the opportunity, through the exercise of freedom of the will, to win salvation.

Wesley emphasized preaching, not ritual or ceremonial. He is said to have delivered as many as eight hundred sermons a year for half a century, at any and all hours of the day, and to have travelled between four and five thousand miles a year. He was an indefatigable pamphleteer and letter writer, and wherever he went, he distributed his religious tracts. Then he organized classes among his followers to keep the flame burning which his sermons had ignited in the hearts of his listeners. Despite the reputation of many later Methodists as fiery exhorters, John Wesley was essentially a calm and unemotional preacher, who rarely appealed to fear. Like Nast, Wesley was a scholar, with a good university education. He travelled about in a coach fitted out with bookshelves so that his reading would not be interrupted, and he issued about four hundred publications during the long years of his activity.

For his faith and his convictions, he braved every form of insult and abuse.

Wesley preached faith in the divine Jesus, universal redemption, justification by faith, salvation from sin by grace, and the witness of God's spirit in man, and insisted that religion was a highly personal experience which could come to any man at any time. He made it clear that the blessings of religion were available to the "lower classes" as readily as to the more fortunately situated, and he was determined to devote his life to being an evangelist among the poor. He gladly would have remained in the Anglican church, but that organization excluded him from its fold.

English Wesleyanism had a significant effect upon the political, social, and economic history of the country, and some have claimed that Methodism helped save England from a cataclysmic upheaval at the time of the French Revolution. Wesley's religion came to grips with the problems of the masses who were suffering from the industrial and agricultural transformation that was going on in the British Isles, and it was concerned primarily with the sudden concentration of population in the large towns and in the northern counties of England. The accelerated mobility of the English population had aroused unrest and dissatisfaction among those who suffered from suddenly being forced out of their familiar environment, and in the best of Englishmen, it stimulated intellectual curiosity about some of the fundamental problems of life and an interest in movements and organizations to alleviate human suffering. Since both church and state had ignored these problems for too long a time, Wesleyanism found a ready-made opportunity to preach a gospel of personal salvation which appealed to the neglected masses and tried to make them experience religion as an overpowering emotion rather than just an intellectual exercise.[1]

Methodism also was a protest against eighteenth century deism, which rejected revealed religion and left the Deity "fenced off from mankind by the laws of nature." Wesleyanism stressed the possibility of intimate communion with a very personal God, the doctrine of free choice, and the possibility of becoming sanctified and achieving Christian perfection. Methodists reacted against the sterile dogma and empty formalism of the churches and appealed to the individual conscience to discard dead theology and ceremonial for a vital religion of experience. The only condition necessary for salvation was a sincere desire to flee from the wrath to come and to seek salvation from sin. Such a state of mind and soul could be achieved by "conversion," a phenomenon which would occur at a certain time and place, usually after a period of anguished searching of heart and soul and a wrestling for forgiveness. After a period of excessive emotionalism, it was expected that the convert would find peace and joy. Conversion then could be followed by sanctification, through God's spirit working in man and leading him to forswear all worldly vanities and pleasures and demonstrate that he had achieved salvation by his everyday personal conduct toward his fellow man.

Early Methodism was not primarily interested in moral and social reforms, as such, but in changing the individual through his personal religious experiences. If enough individuals were converted to God's ways, improvements in the social order were bound to follow. The Methodists preached their gospel in the prisons as eagerly as in their chapels. They founded Sunday schools, organized classes and held "love feasts" among their followers. Especially in America, they

perfected a circuit rider system which performed many functions other than religious, including bringing medical aid to
the ill.[2] It must also be remembered that originally Methodists
took no fees for marriages, baptisms and funerals, and collected
no pew rents from those who came to worship in their chapels.
Moreover, their rigorous church discipline imposed strict
standards of conduct, including regulations against usury.[3]

It is true that many Methodists preached primarily to the
nerves of their listeners, and a psychologist would have much
to say in this connection about crowd psychology, the appeal
to fear impulses, and the release of suppressed emotions and
inhibitions, but the fact remains that Methodism proved to
be one of the most significant social and religious movements
of the last two centuries. It should be added that Wesley,
like Nast, did not like the violent physical phenomena aroused
by the muscular Christianity of many of their brethren and
did their best to keep them within reasonable bounds.

The influence of German pietism on Wesley is a matter
of historical record and is another factor which helps to explain
the close affinity Nast always felt with him. Like Wesley, the
German sectarians protested against ecclesiastical formalism
and stressed the possibility of an inner regeneration, and the
" priesthood of all believers." The Moravians, for example,
talked about an " inner light " which would guide all men,
rejected predestination for " free grace," and organized conventicles, class meetings, and prayer meetings to strengthen
the faith of the brethren. In the winter of 1735-36, John
and Charles Wesley crossed the Atlantic with a company of
eighty Salzburgers and twenty-seven Moravians, on their way
to Georgia, where John Wesley was to serve as a chaplain and
missionary in Savannah and Charles, on the staff of Governor
James Oglethorpe. The two brothers were tremendously im-

pressed with the piety of their travel companions, especially with the complete serenity of the Moravians during a violent ocean storm, and they later testified that by these experiences they were "taught the way of the Lord more perfectly."

John Wesley had learned German, travelled in Germany, and spent some time at Herrnhut, the center of the Moravian faith. He knew the writings of Jakob Böhme, the mystic, and attended Peter Böhler's religious services in London and received instruction from him. He had great respect for the Moravian organization and its charitable activities, although he did not accept Pietism in its entirety. Both Wesleys were deeply moved by the singing of the German sectarians and may have derived from them their appreciation of the importance of hymns as a vital part of their own religious exercises. Charles Wesley wrote over six hundred hymns for the Methodist church. Many of their themes and melodies he borrowed from the *Herrnhuter Gesangbuch* and other German sources.

John Wesley attributed his conversion, which occurred at 8:45 p. m. on May 24, 1738, to Böhler's influence. He describes in his journal just how the change in his life came about at a meeting of the Aldersgate Street Society which he attended and how fear and anxiety suddenly gave way to joy and love, which had its center in God. Here again psychologists might want to comment on the suppressions and inhibitions of Wesley's youth and other inner conflicts and mental discords which were finally resolved by a complete acceptance of religion. But whatever the psychological explanation, the " re-orientation of the psyche " which occurred in Wesley was so important that the historian Lecky believed it marked "an epoch in English history." [4]

The techniques and church polity developed by the early

leaders of Methodism have remained virtually unchanged for two centuries. Conversion remains the heart of the religious experience. It is an act of self-surrender by which guilt and fear and sin may be replaced by a light and a peace that comes from on high. It cannot be denied that the experience was often accompanied by great emotional strains as the mind and body of the penitent struggled with the forces of evil, but the indispensable prerequisites for true conversion were genuine repentance, faith in Christ crucified as a personal saviour, and a realization that God forgives all sins for Jesus' sake, so that man may be reborn, to use Nast's words, to a life of justice, and become "the heir of God and co-heir with Jesus in glory." [5]

Revival meetings were a vital part of Methodism, and reached their highest pitch in America, although they were by no means unknown in other countries. They generally produced intense emotional excitement, and even temporary physical collapse of the converts, as preachers graphically described how man had to choose between damnation to an everlasting hell or salvation for a life of glory in the church. Revival preachers, generally without book-learning or much knowledge of theology, led their hearers back and forth between hell and heaven with eloquent and often violent outbursts of pulpit oratory, and veteran revivalists like Peter Cartwright had little use for "the sapient, velvet-mouthed, downy D. D.'s" of later days.

At revivals, people felt they were being "delivered" from sin. Many saw heaven open and heard heavenly music, as well as the shrieks and cries of the damned. The cries of the penitents for mercy sometimes were so loud that preachers had to stop exhorting and turn the gathering at once into a prayer meeting. William James described such experiences as "the psychology of self-surrender," and in some cases, the penitents' "state of temporary exhaustion" no doubt was a factor in their conversion. Revivals remained a central feature of Methodism, and in the vulgar and often brutal frontier society of early America, they frequently had great effect for good.

The camp meetings which were the scenes of many of the most successful "awakenings" have been described many times, and frequently with an overemphasis on the bizarre. People did fall on the floor, got the "jerks," or lay pale and motionless, or fainted, wept, screamed, and went into convulsions. The noise of this kind of "muscular Christianity" could be heard for considerable distances, and these manifestations of an overwrought religious experience were especially common on the frontier, but they were not limited to American Methodist meetings. Wesley, like Nast, had to endure these strange phenomena, although they disliked such violent physical demonstrations. Bishop Asbury, on the other hand, was undisturbed and welcomed such testimonies to the power of religion. Exhorters sometimes were surprised by their own effectiveness. They did no "book preaching" from manuscript, but shouted, gestured, as Lincoln said, "as if they were fighting bees," roared with joy, or broke out in sobs and tears. Brevity was not one of the characteristics of their exhortations. From the point of view of modern child psychology, one cannot help wondering what permanent damage may have been done to little children whose parents brought them to hear such gruesome descriptions of hell and the damned, and the warning that the end of the world might come at any moment.

The camp meeting had a special appeal for frontier communities, where people were lonely and had few neighbors and eagerly went miles to see new faces. Moreover, hell-fire was not too frightening to men and women who had to live dangerously every day of their lives as they battled the forces of nature and the wilderness. The great open-air meetings were full of drama. Huge crowds assembled in a great clearing to listen to a battery of leather-lunged, pulpit-thumping orators. Tents were set up on the periphery of the huge crowd, campfires blazed, and candles, lanterns and torches shone through the black night and cast their eerie shadows over the dark forest. Camp meetings often were a steadying influence for a rough frontier community, and they provided relief from the emptiness and loneliness, the cultural barren-ness, the social isolation, and the monotony of daily life, and served as a safety valve for pent up fears and hopes. Politicians attended these meetings in order to garner votes, merchants to sell their goods. Others came simply to enjoy a fellowship with others, around open fires where men and women, who probably had never met before, cooked their common meals,[6] and joined in the hymn singing, which was one of the most effective revival techniques. Some of the songs were mere doggerel, without the dignity appropriate to a religious occa-sion, and their effectiveness must have depended somewhat on the existing state of tension, excitement and expectancy, as people responded to the rhythm of the music in a kind of " singing ecstasy."

Finally, something must be said about the effective church polity which Methodism developed. Certain disci-plinary requirements were imposed upon all members of the church, and they were set down in detail in a book of disci-pline and regulations. They were enforceable, through judicatory processes, from the individual church up through the General Conference of the Methodist church and its highly centralized hierarchy.

At the bottom of the scale of the preaching hierarchy were the "licensed exhorters," whose authority derived from the supervising minister and whose appointment depended on recommendations from the local class or its leader. Exhorters were required to serve a probationary period, after which, upon examination by a conference of ministers in the district, they could be admitted to "full connexion." Meantime they could preach but not administer the sacraments. The local preacher came next in the hierarchy, and then the circuit rider. The latter, whose story was part of the romance of the American frontier and whose annals are as interesting and inspiring as those of the early Jesuit Fathers in America, usually rode over large circuits. He braved all the rigors of outdoor life and the dangers of a wild and undeveloped country, as he went about on horseback, with cape, umbrella and saddlebags, to carry the Methodist gospel to the most isolated areas, and nurse the seeds he had sown into full-blown churches. The arrival of these messengers of the cross was a great social occasion on the frontier, and people came for miles around to listen to the preaching, to have their children baptized and to partake of the sacrament. The circuit rider usually lived at the homes of his fellow Methodists; he brought them books, and pills for their ailments, and he gave them some news of the outside world and frequently was able to exercise a restraining influence upon a raw and lawless frontier, where gambling, fighting and intemperance were all too prevalent. Many of the circuit riders had little education, but they could hardly be described as ignorant, and some of them were genuinely eloquent. Peter Cartwright, the most famous of the American circuit riders, spent seventy-one years in the saddle. Finally, the Methodist church had its quarterly and annual meetings, and local, district and general conferences, for the transaction of business of all kinds, and in time a considerable number of bishops, who stood at the apex of the hierarchy. The General Conference was the sovereign and supreme law-making body of the church.

This, in brief, was the Methodism that developed in England and spread to America. Ten years before the Declaration of Independence, Methodist missionaries already were roaming the colonies, and Francis Asbury, who had come to America as a volunteer in 1771, was given the status of Wesley's "General Assistant" in 1772. Because of the British origin of most of the early Methodist missionaries in the colonies, and Wesley's known conservatism, which made it impossible for him to accept the American Revolution with equanimity, the Methodists fell into disfavor with many of the patriots and needed to be reorganized after the war.

Wesley always had hoped that Methodist societies everywhere could be kept within the British jurisdiction, and even as part of the Established Church, but, after 1783, he too came to realize the need for a distinctly American church. He deplored the necessity for cutting the ties with England, but was wise enough not to fly in the face of "God's providence." In the winter of 1784-85, the Methodist Episcopal church was organized in New York, the first religious group in the new United States to form an independent, national organization, and Wesley designated Dr. Thomas Coke and Francis Asbury as "joint superintendents for our brethren in North America." In due time, Coke consecrated Asbury a bishop, and the American episcopal hierarchy for Methodism was born. Thereafter, Asbury and his circuit riders roamed far and wide to bring lost sheep into the fold. There was not a single college graduate or ordained minister among them, but they were remarkably successful, and many of the early preachers boasted of being graduates of "Brush College," whose curriculum was limited "to the philosophy of nature and the mysteries of redemption."

Before long, Methodist missionaries crossed the Alleghenies. There was an "Ohio Circuit" as early as 1783, and a "Muskingum and Hockhockin Circuit" by 1800. Asbury himself preached from Maine to Virginia and in the Carolinas, and from the Atlantic Coast to the interior of Tennessee, Kentucky and Ohio. "Methodism came riding into Cincinnati on horseback in the person of Rev. John Kebler in 1798," a presiding elder from the Kentucky district, and a Methodist society was organized there, the Queen City of the West, as early as 1804.[7] Methodism soon outstripped other religions in the West in the number of its communicants. In Ohio, the Methodist church counted among its members such prominent men as Robert Lucas, later governor of both Ohio and Iowa; Edward Tiffin, the first chief executive of the state; Thomas Worthington, a prominent leader in the movement for statehood; John McLean, who became postmaster general and a justice of the United States Supreme Court; Allen Trimble, a future governor; and James B. Finley, a famous Indian agent. But the democratic theology of Methodism appealed to frontiersmen in general, who found its gospel of free will both attractive and useful. The excellent church organization of the Methodists, from class leaders to circuit riders and bishops, accounted for their initial successes as well as for the effective consolidation of their forces into a strong American church.

Some of the early American missionaries had come in contact with the German settlements of Pennsylvania, Maryland, Virginia and New York. A number of Germans were converted, and in time preached the Gospel in German and English, but no separate German organizations were founded in this early period. Jakob Albrecht, a local Methodist preacher in 1790, who "itinerated" among the Germans, might have set up German churches had not Bishop Asbury insisted that all preaching must be in English. Consequently, Albrecht seceded in 1807 from the Methodists to found his own Evangelical Association. Asbury continued to refuse to sanction separate work among the Germans, but relented sufficiently in 1808 to permit Heinrich Böhm to prepare a German translation of the discipline for circulation among German-speaking members.

The Methodist annual conference of 1784 listed 46 circuits and stations in the United States. By 1819, there were 475 stations, 977 travelling preachers, and 281,146 members, over 30,000 of whom were in Ohio. In 1812, 90 delegates from eight annual conferences assembled in New York for the first American General Conference of delegates assembled from throughout the nation.[8]

This was the church, in its doctrines, practices and organization, to which Nast was destined to commit the remainder of his long life. It was well established in the United States and in Ohio when his conversion occurred. In this church he found a completely satisfying spiritual home, and through it he hoped to work among his fellow German immigrants for the salvation of their souls and for their better adjustment to the new country to which they had committed their families and their fortunes.

4

MISSIONARY TO THE GERMANS

Nast's struggle for inner peace finally came to a happy end with his conversion in 1835, while he was a teacher in the preparatory department at Kenyon. In later years, when he had acquired status throughout the United States as the revered patriarch of German Methodism, he was requested to tell the story of his conversion to congregations in both this country and Canada, where his recital of his religious experiences was generally greeted by the faithful with loud amens and halleluliahs. He published an account of his conversion on several occasions in the *Apologete*, and save for a few minor details, it varied little with the passing years.

Nast's health was not good before he went to Gambier, and for part of the time when he was a teacher at Kenyon. During the winter of 1833-34, he had spent some time on a farm near Gallipolis, and in Gallia County he encountered Adam Miller, a Pennsylvania German who had responded to an appeal by Bishop Emory, printed in the *Western Christian Advocate*, for some one who would be able to preach in the German language. According to Miller's account, he heard of young Nast while passing through Zanesville, but actually met him for the first time while the latter was engaged in tutoring several children on a Gallia County farm. Because Miller wanted to improve his German and thought Nast could help him, he took him along on his Point Pleasant circuit, into Virginia, where there were many German settlers. According to one account, Nast spoke to a small Virginia audience following one of Miller's sermons, and told his listeners how he had been reared a Christian, had fallen into doubt and unbelief, and had become a lost soul. That night, when Miller awoke, he found his travelling companion on his knees, engaged in fervent prayer.

In Gambier, Nast had become acquainted with a pious cobbler, John Smith, who took him to a Methodist quarterly meeting in nearby Danville, in Knox County, where the Reverend Adam Poe was conducting revival services at a camp meeting. It was here that Nast was finally sufficiently moved to go forward to the altar. He described how his eyes were suddenly opened to the glory of God, and how he fell on his knees to ask for forgiveness. When all the others had left, he returned alone to the altar, and it was then that he felt "the witness of the spirit" and was "born again." In later years, he commemorated the anniversary of that important day in January of 1835 in several issues of his *Apologete*. "I was filled with joy unutterable and full of glory," he reported. "I was on the Rock." "I did not let the Lord go until he blessed me." At last he was convinced that he had recovered the faith of his boyhood and that his long struggle for salvation was over.

Nast returned to Kenyon to tell his students and the faculty the glorious tidings and prayed with some of them in his room. On January 31, 1835, he was licensed as an exhorter in the Methodist church, receiving his certificate from the Danville quarterly conference. It was signed by A. Goff, and authorized him to exhort, " so long as his Spirit, and practise, accord with the Gospel and the Discipline " of the Methodist church. By July, Nast had advanced to the status of a local preacher, and on September 15, at the age of twenty-eight, he was formally admitted, on trial, to the Ohio Methodist Conference.[1]

As the academic year at Kenyon drew to a close, Nast must have been troubled by the thought that he might soon be unemployed, and in one of his last letters to Rebecca Duncan he referred to his gloomy prospects. Fortunately for him, just at this time a number of influential Methodists were considering the desirability of doing special missionary work among the growing number of German immigrants who were settling in various parts of the country, especially in the farming areas and towns of the Middle West. In later years some of Nast's friends contended that God's providence had provided him for the German work at just the right psychological moment, and he himself was convinced that his career had been foreordained by God, that the German work was guided and directed throughout his lifetime by a divine hand, and that whatever happened to him, good or bad, was in accordance with the divine plan.

As early as 1833, two agents of a Methodist publishing concern had advocated establishing a mission to the Germans of Cincinnati. Early in 1835, Adam Miller wrote to Bishop

Thomas A. Morris, editor of the *Western Christian Advocate*, pointing out that the time was ripe for Methodists to begin working among the German element and that he, Miller, would volunteer to continue the study of the German language, if there were support for his proposal. Morris printed the letter in his journal, with his editorial endorsement. Similar appeals came from St. Louis, stressing the need for German missionaries in the West, where many who wanted to attend religious services did not know enough English to follow the sermon. It was pointed out also that it was the duty of the Methodist church to combat the " spiritual night " which had fallen over many of the recent arrivals from Germany. Many Protestants were drifting like sheep without a shepherd; others were falling into the clutches of " Romanism " or were becoming rationalists and infidels. A number of the German Protestant churches in the United States had not yet established firm synodical connections and lacked a central administration; many preachers were untrained and had not been licensed by any responsible authority, and many frontier settlements were entirely without ministers of the Gospel. Adam Miller called for a vigorous campaign against German rationalism and " the lifeless forms of Christianity " so that the " leaven of an active, aggressive Christianity " might be thrown into the balance against the " mass of moral corruption that was landing on our shores by the hundreds of thousands." [2]

In response to such demands, Nast was appointed by the Ohio Conference in 1835 as missionary to the Germans of Cincinnati. There was some opposition to the proposal, but Bishop Morris and other prominent Methodists, like J. B. Finley, gave it their support. The Methodist Missionary Society agreed to pay Nast one hundred dollars for the year, but was unwilling to make any further commitments until the experiment had proved itself.

Cincinnati had grown from a population of 9,642 in 1820 to nearly 25,000 by 1830, and in 1836, the total reached 38,000. Despite ravages by fire, flood and cholera in 1832, the city was remarkably prosperous. Business from the Ohio canals was growing, and large quantities of corn and grain were sent down the Ohio and Mississippi rivers to New Orleans. The culture of the vine had become profitable, whiskey distilleries were flourishing, and the slaughtering of hogs had become such a prominent feature of the town's economy that Cincinnati became known far and wide as " Porkopolis." A number of railroads were chartered in the 1830's with Cincinnati as a key point, and by 1835, fifty stages and sixty mails arrived in the city each week. Manufacturing, including a prosperous ship-building industry, was developing steadily, and coal was replacing wood as fuel. A Young Men's Mercantile Library was founded in 1835 and also an anti-slavery society. Cincinnati already was something of a cultural center, its publishing houses were turning out many books and periodicals, and in 1838, the Academy of Fine Arts was organized.

Although Cincinnati still was primarily a Yankee city, populated from the East, its German population was multiplying rapidly, and by 1840 the city was 23 per cent German. Several German newspapers were published there before 1840, including the Catholic *Wahrheitsfreund*, established in 1837, and the *Cincinnati Volksblatt*, founded the year before and for a time the only German-language daily in the United States. Nast was one of its faithful readers. A number of influential Germans had founded a German Society in 1834, and a German militia company, known as the Lafayette

Guards, was organized two years later. Singing societies sprang up wherever Germans settled in this country, and a movement was started to establish German schools and to have German taught in the public schools. By 1838, an Ohio law permitted school trustees to respond to local demands to teach German in the public schools. Several prominent German residents of Cincinnati already were active in local politics, and by 1840 the German vote was regarded as important by both political parties.[3] The district north of the Miami Canal, which entered Cincinnati from the northwest, and which became known as "over the Rhine" because of its predominantly German population, was growing fast. Here, after 1840, beer and concert halls and beer gardens flourished in the densely populated German section, and here also many of the great breweries for which Cincinnati became famous were located. Many of the Germans "over the Rhine" were Catholics from south Germany and the Rhine country.

This was the Ohio River city to which Nast was assigned and to whose German element he addressed his religious appeals. His task was not easy. The Germans, he testified, "are not like those who hear the word and, anon, with joy receive it. . . . They will not lay their hands to the Gospel plough until they have fully made up their minds."[4] To many Germans the very name "Methodist" was a symbol of that gloomy Puritanical Sabbatarianism which they hated as an invasion of their personal liberty, and for which they would substitute the joys and pleasures of the Continental Sunday which they had enjoyed in the fatherland. Because Nast found it difficult to get his fellow countrymen to come to public meetings, he went from house to house, ringing doorbells, exhorting whenever he found some one willing to let him in, and distributing religious tracts. He found that many Germans were held "captive by the Romish priests," while others were contaminated by a rationalism which reduced the "doctrines of our holy religion . . . into a mere system of outward morality," and that men were being nourished "not with the sincere milk of the Gospel and the grace of God but with the beggarly elements of human philosophy." Like Wesley in England, Nast found that religion was rarely presented "to the unlearned other than as a dead skeleton in the form of a catechism." [5]

As a young missionary, he encountered many other difficulties, and strange as it may seem, he had to overcome an embarrassment about preaching in the German language. "Nor was I able to talk the language of Canaan in German very well," he wrote later, "for I was converted in English." He also found it impossible to attract an audience by singing, for he was not a good singer; but this deficiency, he hoped, would some day be corrected in heaven. Moreover, he was naturally shy and much of an introvert and lacked many of the qualities of the rough and ready evangelist who could make an immediately popular appeal. If he managed to get a few listeners assembled in one place, he frequently found that a number walked out before he had half finished his sermon. Sometimes rotten eggs and plugs of tobacco were thrown at him, and disturbances were created by rowdies and drunkards inside and outside the meeting place. On several occasions, a pig or a cow was driven under the meeting house where he was preaching, and on another occasion a rooster was brought into the church and let fly during the sermon. Once someone slipped behind him and cut his coat-tails with a scissors. While preaching in a saloon, his listeners, one by one, tiptoed out until he was finally left standing alone and talking to himself.

Nast preached first in a more formal way, in a Sunday School room of Wesley Chapel on Fifth Street, to an audience of twenty-four Germans and a dozen English. Later he spoke in schoolhouses, often outdoors, in fact anywhere where he could entice people to stay long enough to hear what he wanted to say. He distributed Methodist tracts at the entrance to beer gardens and in saloons and on public highways, and he made many house to house visits. Occasionally, he was invited to preach in a home by its hospitable and friendly occupant. The press of Cincinnati, and particularly the German-language papers, unmercifully ridiculed him, his message and his methods, but at least they took notice of his work and gave publicity to his activities. When he was most discouraged, he testified that he received almost daily support from Bishop Leonidas Lent Hamline, whose style of preaching and writing Nast tried to emulate.[6]

At the end of a year of effort, Nast could report that he had organized a class of twelve, but that he had only three actual converts. One was Caroline Müller, another was Eduard Hoch, who acted as a sort of bodyguard for the harassed missionary and whose son became governor of Kansas, and the third was John Zwahlen, a native Swiss, who deserves to be remembered as one of the co-founders of German Methodism in the United States.[7]

When his initial appointment expired, Nast was given a new commission by the Ohio General Conference as a missionary to the Germans of all Ohio. Now he had to ride horseback over a circuit of some three hundred miles and was expected to cover his twenty-five preaching appointments once in every five weeks. The circuit included Columbus, Newark, Mt. Vernon, Danville, Loudonville, Mansfield, Galion, Bucyrus, Worthington and Delaware. His pioneer efforts in a number of these places blossomed into the establishment of German Methodist churches. In all, he rode about four thousand miles during the year. He had so little experience with horses that he regularly prayed the Lord to help him manage his steed. The number of actual converts, "ready to join us in the pilgrimage to Zion," remained pitifully small.

In 1837, the Conference sent Nast back to Cincinnati as the German missionary to the city and its environs and thus relieved him of the arduous duty of riding a circuit. Now he was able to conduct regular German services on Sunday afternoons at Burke's Chapel on Vine Street, in the heart of a German section, and in Asbury Chapel on Upper Main Street, in a frame structure known as "Brimstone Corner." He started a Sunday school and by the summer of 1838 was able to organize the first German Methodist society in Cincinnati with twenty-six charter members.

Many of the stalwarts of German Methodism in the United States were among Nast's early converts. By the end of 1838, John Zwahlen had a congregation of eighty-three members in Wheeling, where he built the first German Methodist church in the United States, and perhaps in the world. Peter Schmucker, a former Lutheran minister, was another of Nast's early converts. Schmucker distributed Methodist tracts on river boats at the wharves, and on the streets, and had a successful career as a missionary in the Middle West and South. He founded missions in Louisville and New Orleans and other cities, and conducted a number of successful revivals. In Louisville, he encountered the hostility of the German-language press, of the "Romanists" and the "grog sellers" and drinkers, and the German rabble stoned his church.

In 1838, Nast was in Pittsburgh for a two-week preaching mission, during which he preached every day. Among his converts was Engelhardt Riemenschneider, who had learned the tailoring trade in Germany. He had come to the United States as a young man and proceeded on foot from Baltimore to Wheeling, and after a long struggle, at the age of twenty-three, he was "awakened" by Nast in Pittsburgh. He became a Methodist preacher, preached in many Ohio towns, and worked with especial effectiveness among the Swiss and Alsatians in the Captina Hills of Monroe County, where he helped develop the Monroe Mission. In 1850, Riemenschneider returned to Germany to carry on the work there.

One of Nast's best known early converts was Ludwig Sigmund Jacoby. He was of German-Jewish stock; he was baptized a Lutheran in 1835 and married a woman who had been reared as a Catholic but who renounced her church to go with her husband. In 1839, he came to Cincinnati, heard Nast preach, visited him in his home, and was converted to Methodism. His career will be considered in greater detail in a later chapter.[8]

From the large number of Nast's early converts, each of whom became important in the movement, it is difficult to make additional selections, although certainly such important figures as Wilhelm Ahrens, Franz Nuelsen and Michael and Leonhard Mulfinger would be included. Their names, with many others, appeared later among the contributors to Nast's *Apologete*. Leonhard Mulfinger was one of the pioneer heroes of German Methodism, and when his son, Julius A., wrote his biography, Nast wrote a foreword in which he referred to his venerable colleague as "the Nestor of German Methodism in the Northwest."[9] The list of converts also included several curious and unstable characters, among whom Wilhelm

Keil was probably the most extraordinary. Keil came to Pittsburgh in 1836 to practice a kind of pow-wowing medicine. He was converted to Methodism by Nast in 1838 and preached in Ohio and Pennsylvania until he was expelled from the church, according to his own account, for objecting to having pastors paid a salary. Thereupon he became an independent preacher and a mystic and finally set up a new faith in which he was the " Central Sun " and his followers " the princes of light." He established two communistic settlements in Missouri and Oregon.[10]

5

THE EARLY YEARS OF GERMAN METHODISM

The seeds sowed by Nast and his early associates were scattered throughout the nation, from the Atlantic to the Pacific, south to New Orleans and Texas, and finally into Canada and Latin America, and by missionaries across the seas to Europe and Asia.

In 1840, there were only 20 German Methodist preachers in the whole United States; in the next decade, the number increased rapidly and the church membership reached nearly 10,000; by 1858, the membership again had doubled.[1] Five years before the Civil War, the German work was organized into 15 districts, with 138 churches and 59 parsonages, 165 full-fledged German circuit riders, 24 others who travelled under the supervision of presiding elders, and 120 local preachers. There were over 200 German Methodist Sunday schools, with a pupil enrollment of nearly 7,500. As early as

1844, the German missions, located in the various Methodist conferences, were being systematically combined into German districts under presiding elders. The Ohio Conference had two such districts, presided over by C. A. Döring and Peter Schmucker, and similar progress was being made in the organization of the German work in Missouri, Illinois and several other states. Shortly after the Civil War, there were three German conferences, a Central, a Southwest, and a Northwest, and as early as 1848, Nast and Jacoby went as German delegates to the Methodist General Conference. Before Nast died, seven other German conferences had been formed, and in 1905, the San Francisco Conference was added to the list. By that time, the total German membership was 63,000; there were 20,000 Methodists in Germany and Switzerland, largely because of the work of missionaries sent abroad from the United States; 350 German Methodist books had been published in America; and there were 880 German churches and 475 parsonages in the United States, with an estimated property value of $4,500,000.

The number of faithful souls who helped develop the evangelical work which Nast had initiated runs into the hundreds. The story of only a few of the pioneers of German Methodism can be retold here and only as illustrative of the similar experiences of many others. Some of the first German Methodist congregations were started in private homes, others were born in schoolhouses or in the churches of American Methodist congregations. In Chillicothe, Ohio, the first Methodist society met on the lower floor of the Masonic Hall. In other localities, the Germans rented a church and held their services in the afternoons. In Covington, Kentucky, they bought a little Baptist church for $1,100. In Terre Haute, Indiana, they took over a building from the Presbyterians;

in Spraytown, Indiana, from the Lutherans. A number of congregations progressed through several stages, from meetings in a blockhouse, to a frame structure and finally to a brick church. In Evansville, Indiana, Schmucker held the first meeting of his group in a tavern whose owner he had converted; in Goshen, Indiana, the German Methodists rented a meeting place from the Swedenborgians. In Allegan, Michigan, the congregation of Johann Valentin Jahraus secured the use of the lower floor of a rat-infested jail, then moved into the Court House, and finally into a little church valued at over $2,000. In Columbus, Ohio, meetings were held in 1843 in a schoolhouse, and later in a fire station.[2]

Many early church buildings were primitive unpainted wooden structures, without decoration of any kind, with walls completely bare and seats that were hard and uncomfortable. In the front of the room there generally was a platform, five to six feet long, with a bench on which three or four preachers could sit. On the pulpit lay the Bible, a hymnal and a copy of the Discipline. Many early churches had no organs, carpets or pictures, and ministers frequently had to "line out the tunes" for the hymns they wanted their congregations to sing because there was no musical instrument to indicate the melody. Subscriptions to building funds for the early churches often were in the form of gifts of lumber, store goods and sundries. Obviously, donations of this kind depreciated and deteriorated substantially if too much time elapsed between the collection of pledges and actual building operations. On a number of occasions newly established congregations were weakened by internal dissensions. In Berea, Ohio, in 1863, for example, twenty-eight joined the church, but only fifteen were deemed acceptable. The rest were dropped "because of love of the dance," unseemly controversies with other members, or other acts considered sinful under a strict application of the rules of the Methodist Discipline.

Many pioneer preachers in the German Methodist ministry had little formal education with the exception of the thorough elementary training they had received in the schools of Germany. Many were humble artisans, who had been converted in the United States and licensed to preach. George Adam Reuter, for example, a native of Bavaria who was licensed to preach in 1849, was a cooper by trade. Johann Plank was a shoemaker from Hesse-Darmstadt, who was converted by a circuit rider, licensed, and given various preaching assignments in the Middle West. After years of preaching he retired to a farm, and throughout his career he engaged in the practice of medicine as a kind of second vocation.[3] Philipp Kuhl, who belonged to the Reformed church in Germany, was a sign painter before he became a Methodist preacher in the South.[4] W. Hemminghaus, a Hanoverian, was a watchmaker by trade. Johann Jahraus, Heinrich Lich and Konrad Böcklein were tailors; Charles E. Helwig was a carpenter; Döring had been trained for a business career in Germany before coming to the United States in 1836 but, unlike so many of his German Methodist brethren, had graduated from Allegheny College before he began to preach. Johann Heinrich Liebhart attended Heidelberg but worked with pick and shovel in the United States before he entered the ministry and later became the editor of several German Methodist journals. Heinrich Kastendick and Frederich Magdanz were blacksmiths, Paul Quattlander was a house painter, and Jakob Rothweiler learned the machinist trade.

A considerable number of the early German Methodist ministers were recruited from other denominations. Schmucker originally was a Lutheran; Adam Miller belonged to a family of Amish Mennonites of Maryland.⁵ Johann Geyer was a Dunkard. Zwahlen was a member of the Swiss Reformed church. George A. Breunig was a Catholic who became a Lutheran before he turned to Methodism. George Danker left his Lutheran pastorate in Marietta, Ohio, to join the German Methodists. Dr. R. A. W. Bruehl left the Catholic church, became an avowed atheist, took part in the unsuccessful German Revolution of 1848, and thereafter fled to England. When he settled in the United States, he was converted to Methodism in 1851 and became a colporteur of German Methodist tracts and an employee of The Methodist Book Concern of Cincinnati.⁶ Nikolaus Nuhfer was a Bavarian Catholic who was converted to German Methodism in 1842. Jakob Kindler, one of the first German Methodist preachers in Marion, Ohio, had a similar Catholic background, and Paul Brodbeck, from Baden, left the Catholic church when he married a Methodist and accepted his wife's faith. The number of converts from Catholicism was relatively large and included an occasional Roman Catholic priest.⁷

German Methodists adopted the circuit rider system of their American brethren along with other features of the American church. By this extraordinarily effective institution, they were able to keep in touch with the frontier communities, where people were constantly on the move. Though it imposed many hardships, the circuit rider system had the advantage of distributing the available preaching talent more equitably and by enforcing a policy of rotation made it impossible for individual preachers to build up mere personal influence with their parishioners and prevented congregations from selfishly clinging to one minister, thus depriving others of his talents. The circuit rider preacher was expected to strike few permanent roots and to feel at home anywhere.

The salaries of German circuit riders were pitifully low, at the outset, and rarely exceeded a hundred dollars a year, although this stipend was often augmented by gifts of food and usable goods. The horse was the circuit rider's best friend, but the rider had to personally feed and curry and take care of him, when he stopped overnight, generally at some farmhouse where the owner was friendly to Methodism. Sometimes the circuit rider had to sleep under the open sky, holding on to the reins of his horse and using the saddle for his pillow and his cape as a blanket. Neither the heat of the summer nor the cold of winter were expected to keep him from making his appointed rounds. The hazards to health were great; primitive blockhouses were cold; thunderstorms drenched the riders to the skin; and frequently the streams they had to ford were swollen by floods. Few escaped the " ague," the chronic malady of the frontier, and many developed throat ailments which forced them to give up preaching prematurely. As the settlement of the country developed, the circuit rider finally was able to cover part of his route by stagecoach or canal boat.

The rugged schedule of the itinerant preacher left no room for personal vanities or much concern for personal comfort. In the 1840's and 1850's, German Methodist missionaries, like their American brethren, went out to the remotest frontier to hunt up isolated German families or settlements, to bring them the benefits of religious services conducted in the only language they could as yet understand. The itinerant preacher gave them Methodist tracts to read and encouraged them to organize classes for the further study of the basic tenets of Methodism. In many places, the circuit rider and the exhorter met with a cool reception and in a few instances encountered even physical violence from scoffers who came to break up their meetings.[8]

The saddlebags of the circuit rider were stuffed with a variety of materials. Besides a few articles of clothing, they contained Methodist publications, the Bible, a copy of the Discipline, the Methodist hymnal, perhaps Fletcher's *Appeal* and some of the works of John Wesley, a miscellany of German books, and a variety of tracts shipped out by the Methodist Book Concern (established in 1828), which was systematically producing German tracts by the late 1840's. The circuit rider offered this printed material for sale to interested customers and, at the same time, solicited subscriptions for such church publications as the *Methodist Magazine*, the *Ladies Repository*, and Nast's *Der Christliche Apologete*. Out of the thickly stuffed saddlebags also came the homeopathic pills which German circuit riders dispensed for whatever ailments they encountered on their travels. Thus, their contributions to life on the frontier were not limited to religion but included much that had to do with the physical well-being and the cultural status of the people they encountered.

Toward the end of the nineteenth century, many of the early German circuit riders wrote accounts of their early experiences, and Nast gave considerable space in his *Apologete* to their reminiscences. Several volumes could be filled with such recollections, but several examples, selected at random, must suffice to illustrate the hardships early circuit riders had to endure and the unwavering devotion with which they carried out missionary duties, which they all agreed were specially blessed by God.

Engelhardt Riemenschneider, a well-known name in the history of German Methodism in the United States, began his career in the United States by carrying bricks for seventy-five cents a day. By 1841, he was riding the North Ohio District, a circuit which included many stations between Delaware and Toledo. He covered the five-hundred-mile area once every three weeks, and preached ten to twelve times a week. When he preached in schoolhouses, he sometimes had to walk four or five miles just to get permission to use the building. Then he had to lay his own fires and bring his own candles to light the meeting place. His initial salary was a hundred dollars a year, with no allowance for expenses.[9] In the Captina Hills of Monroe County, he often walked as much as thirty miles to get to his preaching station. In this area, he covered the two-hundred-mile circuit on foot, for he had neither horse nor wagon when he began preaching the Gospel in Monroe County. It was Riemenschneider who brought Ludwig Nippert's mother into the Methodist fold at a New Year's prayer meeting and, later, converted her son, an outstanding figure in the history of German Methodism both in this country and abroad.[10]

Jakob Haas was an Alsatian who came to the United States in 1830. His first assignment as a Methodist preacher took him to Iowa, where he travelled nearly a hundred miles each week and preached every day for an annual salary of $175.

In 1846, H. Köneke, another veteran German Methodist, wrote from St. Louis to describe his harrowing experiences for the readers of the *Apologete*. On one occasion, when he left home, three of his children were seriously ill with scarlet fever. After riding twenty-one miles his horse became lame and he had to go on by stagecoach. After another three miles, the coach broke down and the passengers were loaded into a farmer's wagon, which carried them thirty-eight miles farther along their route. Where Köneke found lodging for the night, a Methodist loaned him a horse to continue his journey, and he had to ride bareback for another ten miles, through the hot, dusty countryside. He became ill, but finally reached Versailles, Missouri, only to find that the place of the quarterly meeting which he wanted to attend had been shifted, and so he had to travel another twenty miles. For two nights he was without sleep and one of them he sat up in a chair all night long battling bedbugs. On the return trip of this exhausting journey he fell twice from his horse and tore his clothes and lost his way and had to spend a night in the woods. When he finally reached home, he found that his children had recovered from scarlet fever but that his wife was confined to her bed with a badly infected gall bladder. His account for the *Apologete* ended with the plea, " Remember me in your prayers." [11]

Karl Stückemann was the first German preacher to enter " Bleeding Kansas." In 1858, he set out from Leavenworth on a pony to seek out the German settlers in that territory who lived twenty-five or thirty miles apart. He had to ford a swollen stream, and his clothes and saddlebags became dripping wet. He found shelter in the hut of an Indian squaw, who built a fire to dry out his clothes, spread buffalo robes for him to rest upon, and cooked him a meal. Such hospitality by a friendly Indian was in sharp contrast to the hostile reception Methodist preachers frequently received from their German countrymen, who either refused them lodging altogether or made them sleep in their corn crib.[12]

The experiences of Köneke and Stückemann could be duplicated many times, but German Methodist missionaries doggedly continued on their missions until their travels finally extended as far west as California and Methodist societies and churches had been established from the Atlantic to the Pacific coast.

Accounts of the adventures and sacrifices of the circuit riders only rarely refer to the experiences of their wives, whose burdens were often heavier than those of the husbands. The women had to remain at home, anxiously awaiting the return of their men, and never certain what might happen to them on the sparsely settled frontier. Moreover, the wives had to feed and clothe a growing family on their husbands' pitifully low salaries. They bore children in lonely peril, in exposed parts of the frontier where the nearest neighbor might be many miles away. Sometimes a baby was born, died and was buried before the father returned from the circuit. Furthermore, ministers' wives were not permitted to indulge in any personal vanities, however innocent and harmless. They were expected to dress in extremely plain clothes, most of which they had to make themselves. Rings, with the exception of a wedding band, were considered worldly baubles, and on occasion, even these were tossed into the collection plate because women had nothing else of value to contribute to the cause of the Lord. Cosmetics and every kind of frill were frowned upon under the strict discipline of the church, and hats could be decorated with nothing more frivolous than a simple ribbon.

On rare occasions only did the *Apologete* carry accounts of the experiences of preachers' wives. One was the account of a minister's wife from Missouri, who reported the hardship that had befallen her family when the husband lost his horse and saddle, representing an outlay of a hundred dollars, during his second year of service. The hard pressed wife bemoaned what it cost to maintain a horse, recounted the illness of her baby and the disastrous inroads made by a doctor's bill of fifteen dollars upon the family budget of $175. The recital of these misfortunes ended with the statement that the family often was reduced to eating dry bread, " wet with tears." [13]

Another brief narrative is from the widow of H. C. Dreyer, describing the experiences of the family when her husband was transferred from Versailles, Missouri, to Chicago. The family's meager belongings were transported by ox-wagon part of the way, then by river boat up the Mississippi, from St. Louis, and thence by canal to Chicago. When the family arrived in the growing Illinois metropolis, the husband scoured the city in search of lodgings for his family, while the mother waited patiently, sitting on a trunk, with a sick child. Unsuccessful in their search for suitable quarters for the night, the family were given a place to sleep by a brother Methodist, who housed them in one room. They had to purchase water for six cents a barrel, an epidemic of cholera was sweeping the city, and the oldest boy died shortly after they arrived in Chicago.[14]

These are but a few examples from the extensive annals of the devotion and self-sacrifice which mark the work of the early German Methodists, as they persisted, against incredible odds, in carrying out what they believed was their divinely-appointed mission. After years of service, their health had often become affected by the hazards of their occupation, and they found themselves moved to the superannuated list, with no visible means of support from the church which they had served for a number of years. There were no ministers' pensions in the early days, and even in the last years of the German Conference, pensions were inadequate. A pastor who served the Ohio Conference for half a century retired with a pension of $72 a year. Many of the early German ministers suffering from throat ailments aggravated by exposure to primitive, frontier conditions, had to give up preaching long before they had planned to. Those who had been craftsmen before their conversion, might resume their earlier trades. Others thought they could make a living for their families from the land and tried farming. Some sold patent medicines. Jahraus, for example, returned to tailoring but also peddled among his Methodist brethren a "family register," with pictures and Bible verses around the border and ample space for family genealogies, which he had a lithographer design for him. The *Apologete* carried many advertisements from superannuated ministers and asked that their little business ventures be given generous support.[15] But the veterans, who continued to write to Nast in the hope that he would print their letters in the *Apologete*, seldom complained of their lot, and seemed grateful for the opportunities God had given them to carry the Gospel to their German brethren.[16]

The number of complaints was surprisingly small. In 1856, a minister wrote the *Apologete* to describe living conditions on the frontier, where food had to be brought in over many miles of roads so muddy that one could hardly get over them with a horse and where the minister had to repair the parsonage with his own hands and pay for the materials out of his own pocket.[17] In 1863, another minister described his transfer from Roxbury, Massachusetts to Rochester, New York. When he arrived at his new location, one member of his congregation gave him a ham; others gave the family butter and food; and another presented his wife with a dozen brooms, "so she can keep the beautiful palace into which we have just moved" clean. The railroad fare to Rochester was over ninety dollars, which exhausted the gift his former parishioners had given him, and so he began in his new church not only in debt but with his first quarter's salary already mortgaged.[18]

Despite many obstacles and discouragements, German Methodism continued to spread. Missions sprang into life in many states, and as soon as a local society was able to support a pastor, the local church was removed from the list of missions supported by the various conferences. Within a few years after Nast initiated the German work, German congregations were formed in the Middle West. The " Mother Church " of German Methodism in Cincinnati was on Race Street and became known as the Nast Memorial Church. By 1842, Döring had a congregation in New York City. There were several German Methodist churches around Belleville, Illinois, and St. Louis, where Jacoby, in 1841, encountered many of the same hostilities which Nast had experienced in Cincinnati and was attacked in both the Catholic press and the German-language papers controlled by freethinkers and agnostics.[19]

By 1844, plans were well along for building the first German Methodist church in Columbus, Ohio. The following year, a little church was dedicated on Buck Hill, in Monroe County, and by 1852 Toledo had its first German Methodist church. In 1845, the American Bible Society of New York sent two hundred German Bibles and two hundred New Testaments to stimulate the German work in Alabama and other parts of the South, and there were early congregations in New Orleans, Charleston, South Carolina, and other Southern cities.

By 1847, the German work had been organized in six districts. Most of the fifty-six churches were still served by ministers who had little formal training in theology, but who, for the most part, were able to write good German and whose vocabulary grew rapidly to include many theological terms. They counted on the fervency of their prayers and the fire of their exhortation to compensate for their lack of advanced study. It would be possible to compile almost a complete chronological list of the establishment of German churches from the files of the *Apologete*, for Nast found space for practically all the accounts sent in to him from the mission field, and before the close of the 1840's he was criticised by some of his readers for giving too much space to such matters. Such accounts "from the field" reported the number of conversions, the organization of Methodist classes, and the struggle to raise enough money to build a church. The story was usually the same, and one can readily understand that some readers found the accounts repetitious and monotonous.[20]

Nast, universally recognized as the man who had planted the seed from which this rapidly expanding German work developed, was in great demand to dedicate new churches in various parts of the country, and his travels sometimes took him away from the editorial rooms in Cincinnati for a week or more at a time, but he enjoyed visiting the various mission fields. In 1840, he was invited to Wheeling to dedicate the first German Methodist church in the United States. Before the end of the decade, he preached in Louisville, St. Louis, and other cities in the Middle West, where new congregations had been organized. In 1846, he dedicated a church known as Ebenezer, in Evansville, Indiana. In 1853, on his way to Pittsburgh, he preached in a number of Ohio cities, in both the English and German languages, and took up collections among the American brethren to help build German churches or pay off the mortgages with which they were encumbered.[21] The following year he preached twice in German and once in English before a new congregation in the Cleveland area and proudly reported that, though small, the little church had a bell tower with a bell weighing 650 pounds. In 1855, he preached on the text "Ye are the light of the world" at the dedication of a new church in Delaware, Ohio, and the next year, he formally opened a church in Dayton.

In 1856, he went to the quarterly meeting in Ann Arbor and to a district meeting in Chicago, using the free passes which railroad companies made it a practice to send to ministers of the Gospel. He preached at a number of places en route. In 1857, he went to the New York Conference, and preached in several eastern cities. Two years later, he stopped in Indianapolis and Fort Wayne, Indiana, and Galena, Illinois, and addressed a General Conference of the Evangelical Association in Naperville, in the hope that the group might be persuaded to merge with the German Methodists. In Chicago, he presided over an all-German ministers' conference, and took a prominent part in all its proceedings.[22]

Nast maintained his strenuous itinerary even during the Civil War, dedicating churches in both the United States and Canada. His expenses for these excursions usually were paid by collections raised among his audiences. On a tour of Wisconsin, he preached with success in Fond du Lac and Watertown, but he found the Germans of Milwaukee particularly difficult to arouse. In 1863, he travelled again through Ohio, Michigan and Illinois, and the following year went west to attend the Southwest German Conference in St. Louis. In 1867, he dedicated a church in Buffalo and attended several German conferences. Just before Christmas he preached the first sermon in a new church in Portsmouth, Ohio, and was happy to find that the ministers of the Lutheran and Reformed churches and his American Methodist brethren were willing to share the platform with him.[23] In 1874, partly on the advice of his physician who recommended a change of climate, Nast took a river boat to New Orleans and went on to Texas to spread the gospel of German Methodism there. Although he encountered some opposition from Southern brethren who disliked his views on the Negro question, the detailed report which he published in the *Apologete* shows he regarded his mission as a great success.[24] As long as health permitted, and until he was a very old man, Nast continued to visit German churches, most of which he regarded as the direct product of the labors he had begun in Cincinnati in 1835, and he was received everywhere as the venerable patriarch of the German Methodist movement.[25]

6

AN IMMIGRANT CHURCH

$\mathfrak{F}$rom its inception, and during most of Nast's lifetime, the German Methodist church was both an integral part of American Methodism and a special agency to serve the needs of one of the large European immigrant groups of the nineteenth century. At the outset German Methodists received substantial financial support from American Methodists who supported their work along with several other missionary projects. German Methodists, of course, conformed to all the regulations of the Methodist church and were subject to the jurisdiction of Methodist bishops in their particular areas. When separate German districts and conferences finally were created, they remained part of the larger American Methodist organizations, and their only unique feature was the use of the German language. There were no doctrinal differences, and the Methodist Discipline applied to all

Methodists, regardless of language or national origin. The German circuit rider system was like that of the English-speaking brethren, and the licensing of exhorters and local preachers, the establishment of local classes, and other practices conformed to the Methodist pattern, which dated from the days of John Wesley, whose theology and evangelizing methods all Methodists accepted.

For the Germans, as for all other Methodists, conversion was the prime objective of their religious appeal, with revivals and camp meetings the chief instruments for achieving this end. The German Methodists counted their converts as eagerly as any other group, and many German churches conducted revivals that continued for a number of weeks. The *Apologete* reported the results of the battle for souls as diligently as a military commander might report the progress of a field operation and used language reminiscent of the military. The forces of righteousness were deployed against the forces of darkness, and camp meetings were described as battlefields or bivouacs from which the armies of the Lord moved out to give battle to the enemy, with "complete victory in sight."[1] A German minister, reporting from the North Indiana District on the "wonderful holy war" going on in his locality, described how "the Prince of Darkness mustered all his forces, with King Alcohol in the van, the Papacy on the right flank, and infidelity on the left . . . but the sword of the spirit is cutting a path through his armies."[2] German Methodist literature referred almost constantly to Jesus as "a triumphant field commander" who maneuvered his forces in the battle against sin with the skill of a commanding general in a major war.[3]

Camp meetings the Germans called *Lagerversammlungen*, and they were a prominent feature of German Methodist procedures. By the time the German church became strong, however, some of the extreme physical phenomena of the conversion process in camp meetings had disappeared. There is no record of a German camp meeting where people fell prostrate to the ground, made wild noises or got the "jerks," but there are many accounts of weeping and shouting for joy, as penitents wrestled with sin and finally found salvation. As late as 1891, the leading German Methodist journal pleaded for the retention of the mourner's bench, and maintained that sinners should be encouraged to break out in tears, loud crying, or shouts of joy. "After earnest, long and difficult wrestling with 'the old Person' and the powers of Satan, why should not the new-born 'child of God' cry out in ecstasy?"[4] In the earlier decades of German Methodism it was common experience to have sinners cry out for forgiveness during the emotional excitement of prolonged camp meetings. In the summer of 1847, Ludwig Nippert preached at a camp meeting near Cincinnati, where it was claimed ten thousand attended the Sunday services. When a six-year-old child died "happy" amid the singing of the multitude, the little corpse was placed before the preacher's platform apparently because many among those present considered the event gave "the camp meeting a special significance."[5]

Every year the *Apologete* announced the season's *Lagerversammlungen*. They were held throughout the country and were especially popular in the Middle West. As early as 1846, the camp meeting near Cincinnati was marked by almost continuous hymn singing and praying and preaching by a half dozen exhorters whose activities continued for an entire week.[6] In the fall of 1856, many "threw themselves prostrate at the feet of Jesus" at a meeting in Jefferson City, Missouri.[7] In 1860, German Methodists marched through the English camp meeting on the Cincinnati camp grounds, singing hymns as they paraded around the tent city, and their American brethren reciprocated by organizing a similar musical procession around the German quarters.

On several occasions, Nast expressed concern about the unusual excitement generated at such meetings, but he was quick to deny charges of rowdyism and disorderly conduct, when they appeared in such papers as Edward Purcell's *Catholic Telegraph*.[8] Although the Germans continued to hold camp meetings to the end of the century, such gatherings gradually lost some of their appeal, and old-time Methodists deplored the decline in interest in the tried and true methods of winning souls to God.[9] In 1872, there was an uproar of protest when the committee in charge of a camp meeting in New York State desecrated the Sabbath by granting licenses to dealers who sold soda water and cigars.[10] On a number of occasions Sunday was turned into a day of confusion and disturbance by the large crowds that milled around the camp meetings and tramped through the dusty streets that divided the rows of tents and houses, which had been rented for the week by their occupants for ten to twelve dollars.[11]

James B. Finley believed the enthusiasm of the Germans for their religion exceeded that of many of their American brethren. "When they sing," he wrote, "they sing lustily; when they pray, they pray with all their might; when they speak in class meeting or love feast, they come right to the point of Christian experience without any circumlocution." [12] But in doctrine, church polity, tactics and procedures, they were indistinguishable from their English-speaking brethren, and even abandoned the confirmation of their children at the age of fourteen, although this was an almost universal practice in Germany and a deeply ingrained tradition with most

German immigrant families. Because Methodism held that the rite did not necessarily involve conversion, German Methodists were ready to give it up.

Most German immigrants had been reared in an atmosphere which regarded Sunday as a day for pleasure and recreation, at least after one's responsibilities to the church had been discharged by attending a morning service or an early Mass. In the United States they found the Puritan Sabbath the exact antithesis of the Continental Sunday which they had known in their homeland. Many European travellers who came to the United States wrote about the boredom of the Sabbath day, and described the quiet of the American Sunday as the quiet of the tomb and pointed out that out of sheer boredom Americans looked forward eagerly for the new week of work to begin. The fact that German Methodists accepted without protest the rigid regulations of their church about Sabbath observance and the sinfulness of most worldly pleasures is one of the most striking evidences of their whole-hearted acceptance of their new-won religion, and many German Methodists were more insistent and uncompromising about the literal application of the Discipline than their American fellow church members.

In 1856, Nast published a piece on the proper way to observe the Sabbath. He advised getting up early and praying for the preacher so that his message might bring a blessing to the congregation. He warned against discussing politics, business, pleasure, or any worldly matter on Sunday, and urged good Methodists to refrain from even thinking worldly thoughts on the Sabbath. He told them not to criticize the preacher and ended his admonitions with a final warning that every one should remember that each Sunday might be his last.[13] When one remembers that a century ago Methodists regarded the accompaniment of a Cleveland church choir with a "wicked fiddle" as a "desecration of the house of God," one can appreciate the many prohibitions contained in the Methodist Discipline, but it is more difficult to understand their unqualified acceptance by European immigrants whose entire cultural and social tradition ran counter to such an ascetic approach to religion.

As early as 1844, German Methodists supported an interdenominational meeting in Columbus, Ohio, attended by two hundred and fifty delegates, including two former governors, which was called to protest against the transaction of business on Sunday and to demand a day of rest for the boatmen on the Ohio canals.[14] Methodists regarded ballets, the theater, dancing and card playing as un-Christian. On a number of occasions, Methodist leaders vigorously denounced the indecencies and immodesty of women's clothing.[15] Nast refused to attend the yearly meeting of Southern Methodists in Nashville because he would not travel on Sunday [16] and was active at a mass meeting of Cincinnati Germans called to demand rigid enforcement of Sunday closing laws. In a lead editorial in the *Apologete*, entitled "Sabbath Peace," he castigated his fellow German immigrants as beer drinkers who flocked to the beer gardens and dances on Sunday and warned that the whole German element in the United States was in danger of losing the respect of their American neighbors by becoming known as "beer representatives."[17] Some years later, Nast denounced the new craze for roller-skating because he thought it promoted too great a propinquity between the sexes.[18] He also deplored the many columns devoted by American newspapers to baseball, to the exclusion of more substantial material on morality and religion.[19] In 1895, the Ohio Annual Conference, with an eye on the Lancaster camp meetings, expressed unalterable opposition " to any and all meetings which open their gates for Sunday trains and Sunday excursions." [20]

German Methodists were as much interested in the crusade for temperance, which they interpreted to mean total abstinence, as any other Methodist group. Nast devoted considerable space in the *Apologete* to prolonged discussions concerning moderate drinking versus abstinence and wrote at length about the question whether the Lord, who created hops and grapes and other ingredients for alcoholic beverages, actually approved of their use for that purpose. It was generally conceded that the use of alcohol for medicinal purposes was an altogether different matter and had the approval of the church. Nast urged his followers to attend temperance meetings and reported the progress of the temperance crusades, especially one launched by the women of Hillsboro, Ohio. He reprinted little temperance stories in the *Apologete* from such publications as the *Temperance Herald* and rated the temperance novel *Mrs. Ben Darby, or the Weal and Woe of Social Life* as important as Harriet Beecher Stowe's *Uncle Tom's Cabin*.[21] The fate of Edgar Allan Poe was held up to his readers as a horrible example of an unrepentant drunkard and sinner.[22] Nast also denounced the German *Sängerfeste* and *Turnfeste* and similar convivial occasions for their immoderate libations to Bacchus and King Gambrinus, and he was especially irritated when, on the occasion of a *Sängerfest* of high musical quality in Cincinnati, free beer was distributed during a parade.[23] When Mrs. Rutherford B. Hayes banished liquor from the White House table, Nast praised her courage.[24] And he argued that there was no proof that the wine at the wedding of Cana was intoxicating.[25]

Nast was frequently at odds with fellow Germans who considered Methodism synonymous with fanatical prohibition and Puritanism. He chided his critics for their narrowly circumscribed conception of personal liberty, which included only the liberty of beer drinkers and saloon keepers. In 1888, when the prohibition question attracted attention in the national campaign, his son Albert was an ardent supporter of the Prohibition party. Nast was disturbed and confused by the emergence of a new party alignment. He hoped temperance reformers might advance their cause by voting either for the Democratic or the Republican party, although he was not sure which party held out the greater promise. As for himself, he found it impossible to desert the Republican party, which he had supported since its formation. He wrote his son, "It will not help the state to carry out prohibition. I cannot help but feel" that a prohibition party "might have an injurious influence on the future of German Methodism." [26] He was alarmed by "the effect upon the German mind" of the protracted argument over the use of fermented or unfermented wine in the communion service, and he was not sure that morality could be established by legislation. In the end, however, he seems to have voted the Prohibition ticket in 1888, and he wrote to Albert to explain his reasons. As a south German, who appreciated an occasional glass of good wine, he doubted the abstract right of government to enact a law forbidding citizens to use relatively harmless beverages, "if not indulged in intemperately," and he was dubious about whether a prohibitory statute could be enforced and whether complete prohibition could guarantee "the permanency of a moral reform." He pointed out, also, that God had not removed all temptation from mankind but had given man a free choice between right and wrong. Hitherto, he had favored regulation rather than total destruction of the liquor business, but now, perhaps because of the persuasive arguments of his son, he satisfied himself that, for a higher moral reason, liquor, the bulwark of the Devil's power, must be destroyed. He hoped God would will the eventual triumph of the Prohibition party, and stressed the use of both ballots and prayers to bring about this moral reform.[27]

The use of tobacco, though an issue of much less magnitude, also agitated many German Methodists. Nast himself was a smoker and got great comfort from the use of what a Virginia planter once called "this bewitching vegetable." In 1856, a correspondent asked the editor why the *Apologete* said so little about the evils of smoking. With his usual frankness and feeling of obligation to his readers, Nast admitted that he smoked and found tobacco good for "certain chronic conditions of his system." He insisted that he used it "as a medicine," and contended that moderate smoking was not a sin. Nevertheless, he admitted that his conscience continued to bother him, and from time to time he had given up smoking for as much as three months.[28] Each time he felt the results had been bad for his system. In 1870, after one of these prolonged experiments with abstinence, his son Albert had to provide medicine and dietetic rules to help his father recover from "the severe effects from having quitted the use of tobacco."[29] Nast's eldest son, William, was delighted when his father resumed his old habit and advised him to take more exercise.[30] The next year Nast went for a cure to the baths in upstate New York, where the doctor put him on a strict diet of cereals, fruit and milk and denied him meat, coffee and tobacco. Nast hoped the cure would rid him of his desire to smoke, but the doctor assured him that at his age it would be unwise to give up tobacco all at once.[31]

Apparently, the use of tobacco remained a live issue with many Methodists, German and otherwise, and on several occasions, the Ohio Annual Conference concerned itself with the problem. In 1881 it condemned the use of tobacco " as an unnecessary and improper indulgence and a reproach to a minister of the Gospel " and demanded strict enforcement of the regulation against it.[32] Three years later, however, the same conference concluded that " a few chronic cases among the older brethren still exist, but there are so few that we may well throw the mantle of Christian charity over their venerable heads in sad remembrance of the strength of their early habits." [33] We may assume that the patriarch of German Methodism, and some of his early German colleagues, were among the few incorrigibles.

With the steady growth of German Methodism it was inevitable that the Germans should agitate for organizations and conferences of their own. At three of the early Methodist conferences and in a communication to the *Western Christian Advocate*, Nast argued for a separate German Methodist body. He encountered strong opposition not only from the English-speaking majority but from a number of his German brethren also, although the latter quickly changed their minds when a bishop began to impose English-speaking presiding elders on German congregations. In 1844, a compromise was worked out which established three German districts, centered at Pittsburgh, Cincinnati and St. Louis, with Döring, Schmucker and Jacoby as their presiding elders. A year later, an Indiana district was added, with Nast as presiding elder. The number of German districts multiplied until there were eighteen, extending from New York to California. As early as 1847, Nast attended the regular Methodist conferences in Ohio, Indiana and Illinois, and he went from the Ohio Conference as the first official German delegate to a Methodist General Conference.

In 1864, after several earlier negative decisions, and largely because of Nast's persistence, the Methodist General Conference finally authorized the formation of four German conferences. In August of that year, the Central German Conference came into being, with eighty preachers and nearly 9,000 members. The newly created body held its first meeting in the Race Street church in Cincinnati, with eighty-four delegates in attendance and with Nast acting as secretary. In September of the same year, the Northwest German Conference was established at Galena, Illinois, with fifty-seven preachers and over 5,500 members. The East German Conference was founded in 1866; the Chicago followed in 1872; the Southern Conference was organized in 1874; the St. Louis in 1877; a Northern German Conference in 1887; the California Conference in 1891; and the Pacific Coast Conference in 1905. At these German gatherings, however, the minutes were kept in English from the outset, because most bishops were ignorant of the German language; but the debates and other conference business were carried on on a bilingual basis. As time went on, even the district conferences of the German church came to transact their business in English, though any member remained free to use the German tongue.

In 1845, twenty-seven German preachers attending the Ohio Conference in Cincinnati asked for a complete Sunday school literature in the German language, and the next year they petitioned for a German edition of Wesley's sermons. By 1848, the Germans of the Ohio Conference had their own tract society. However, in every discussion of the language question throughout the nineteenth century, differences of opinion existed among the Germans themselves. Some wanted to do everything possible to preserve their native tongue as long as possible and hand it on to their children and grandchildren; others believed such a policy would isolate the German group, to its disadvantage, from American Methodism.[34]

In view of the encouraging spread of German Methodism, Nast continued to hope that the German-speaking Evangelical Association, founded by Albrecht early in the nineteenth century, could be brought into the common fold, for actually, there was little difference between German Methodists and Evangelicals in doctrine or practice. Bishop John Seybert of the Evangelicals was thoroughly Wesleyan in his views; his people observed "love feasts," and their services consisted primarily of singing, praying and personal testimony after the Methodist fashion. It would have been difficult to distinguish between the two groups on any important issue, and in the early days, Evangelicals were often known in their communities as Methodists.

In 1843, Nast headed a delegation to the General Conference of the Evangelical Association to plead for closer cooperation and perhaps ultimate union with the German Methodists. He proposed that the two churches unite in publishing standard works on their "common Methodist theology," and also that they pool their resources for the work which both were doing among German immigrants. The reaction to his proposals was extremely cautious, and for twenty years they were not formally revived at any meeting of the Evangelical General Conference.

In 1859, however, Nast went to Naperville, Illinois, as a representative of Methodism, to address the delegates of the Evangelical Association. His special plea was for closer cooperation in the common work Methodists and Evangelicals were doing among German-speaking Americans. Five years later, he headed another delegation to the Association, and in 1867 he attended the latter's General Conference in Pittsburgh. On this last occasion he again stressed the common objective of the two church bodies, namely, "to overthrow the sway over the German people of Romanism, rationalism and every species of Protestant churchism, which, with no protest against the desecration of the holy Sabbath and the fearfully prevailing use of intoxicating drink, pretends to save the people by sacraments." [35] He again broached the subject of a possible merger and proposed that the English activities of the Association be absorbed by the Methodists and the German work of the Methodists be under the control of the Evangelical Association. A committee studied the proposal, and the next year delegates of the Evangelicals attended the Methodist General Conference. They admitted that their own church was " a Methodist body in everything but name," certainly as far as theology and discipline were concerned. The one stumbling block in the way of a merger, however, was a difference in the choice, powers and terms of office of the bishops. Nast suggested leaving the matter to Providence. By 1871 it became abundantly clear that the leaders of the Evangelical Association were not "ripe" for union, although the proposal nevertheless carried in the Evangelical General Conference by a majority of one—an outcome so close that the delegates immediately resolved to await divine intervention and guidance. The movement for union waned rapidly thereafter, although the Evangelicals sent representatives to the Methodist conferences in 1872, 1880 and 1884. Apparently both parties concluded that a merger would be accomplished only if it turned out to be the Lord's will.[36] As late as 1907, Albert Nast, as a fraternal delegate to the General Conference of the Evangelical Association in Milwaukee, repeated many of his father's arguments about the similarities with German Methodists and the desire for greater cooperation.

With the phenomenal spread of German Methodism, Nast would have been less than human had he not speculated about his chances to become the first German bishop of his church, for the election to a bishop's exalted position has been an aspiration of many successful Methodist ministers. In 1864, when separate German conferences were authorized, he wrote his son Albert that there was no danger of his having "to bear the burden of the episcopal office. That question is forever put at rest." [37] Actually, it was anything but a closed issue, both in Nast's mind and in the minds of many of his German fellow ministers. He continued to write in self-denying terms, but he certainly would have accepted election as a Methodist bishop as the crowning achievement of his long and distinguished career, and Albert never abandoned the idea that his father would eventually become a bishop.[38] Whenever the question was discussed in German Methodist gatherings, there were always some German ministers who charged Nast with heterodoxy, because his views on the "doctrine of holiness" deviated somewhat from those of John Wesley, and Jacoby took issue with Nast's *Christology*.

In 1868, the *Apologete* carried several communications urging Nast's election as a bishop. The *Christian Advocate*, on the other hand, opposed a proposal which would divide Methodism according to the national origins of its members,[39] and the Eastern German Conference adopted a resolution specifically objecting to the election of a German bishop. Nast, at the height of the discussion, published a communication on the first page of the *Apologete* from a writer who argued that whoever was chosen as the first German bishop must be a scholar. If this were the most important criterion,

Nast obviously would have little competition from his German fellow ministers.[40] Three years later, he still was discussing the desirability of having a German bishop and arguing that this was a natural consequence which flowed logically from the creation of separate German districts and conferences.

In 1877, the German delegates to the General Conference caucused on the proposal to select a German bishop. When eight different candidates received two votes each, there was no possibility of reaching an agreement on any single candidate. Nast's candidacy was opposed by some delegates on doctrinal matters, such as sanctification, and realizing that he could not be chosen, he proposed Rothweiler as his candidate.[41] In 1888, he wrote his son that some of the English-speaking bishops were hostile toward him and determined "to put me down."[42]

He did not live long enough to witness the decline that was bound to come in the work which he had started, for it was only a matter of time until the forces of assimilation and Americanization could do their work. He undoubtedly would have become reconciled to the unavoidable shrinkage in the membership of the German churches, for he was genuinely interested in the Americanization of the immigrant and always contended that preaching Methodism to the Germans would make them better citizens and help them to become Americanized.

At its height, the German-speaking Methodists in the United States totaled over 63,000 official members. Probably another half million were in some way affiliated with their organizations. The German Methodist church, at the peak of its strength, supported six institutions of higher learning, two theological seminaries, four orphanages, a home for the aged, four hospitals and an extensive deaconess program with a mother house in Cincinnati. The total assets of the German churches eventually reached $6,250,000, and the total conversions in a seventy-five year period were estimated at 250,000.[43]

In the first decade of the present century the German church began to decline sharply. The first World War, with its attendant hysteria toward everything of German origin, hastened the shift from German to English services. By this time, many German churches had become old people's churches, the salaries which they could afford to pay their ministers were lower than those of English-speaking churches, and it became increasingly difficult to attract and train an adequate supply of younger ministers. Young men going into the ministry preferred to attend American seminaries where only English was spoken. The German population became more and more widely scattered, and many cities no longer had isolated German sections, and as a consequence, German and English-speaking parishes began to overlap.

German Methodist stalwarts waged a vigorous rear guard action to keep their churches and conferences alive. They pleaded eloquently and with great emotion with the younger people to learn the language of their fathers and to remain loyal to their family traditions. But their efforts were doomed to fail, as they have failed with every other nationality group in the United States. The decline in German immigration, the refusal of the younger generation to learn and use a difficult foreign tongue, the dearth of candidates for the German ministry, and the advanced age of most of the veterans of German Methodism, led church after church to abandon German for English or at least to give predominance to the latter language in all the church's activities. Gradually, the transition was accepted as natural and inevitable, and indeed, as in accordance with God's will.

The mergers of German and English Methodist conferences began in 1924, and proceeded rapidly. An extra number of the *Apologete*, August 16, 1933, announced the demise of the Central German Conference—the oldest. Two years later, the Eastern German Conference was the only German Conference left, and it expired in the next decade. The German organizations were dissolved into the English. Preaching still went on in the German language in some churches but only to satisfy the religious needs of the older generation, which was rapidly dying out. There are still a few Methodist churches in the United States in which there is preaching in the German language, but for all practical purposes, the work Nast began among the Germans in Cincinnati in 1835 was completely absorbed in American Methodism a century later.[44]

7

THE *APOLOGETE* AS A RELIGIOUS
JOURNAL

Nast was revered as a preacher by thousands who regarded it a rare privilege to listen to the patriarch of German Methodism, and his visits to churches throughout the country brought out large audiences eager to hear the message of salvation from the lips of this devout and sincere servant of God. But neither the composition of his sermons nor his manner of delivery were especially notable. He was not a distinguished pulpit orator. Several of his contemporaries commented upon his rather "heavy tongue," and he never seemed quite at ease on a public platform. Nevertheless, his slightly stooped body, his youthful face, in sharp contrast with the gray head of his later years, made him an appealing figure. His mouth and lips were firm, and his countenance always serious, save for an irrepressible twinkle in his eyes. His face seemed to radiate a simple, trusting piety. His sermons were marked by thoughtfulness, a logical exposition of the text and a practical application of the Gospel to everyday affairs of the individual, but they were not memorable for striking figures of speech or dazzling oratory. There was something rather self-effacing about his manner of delivery. According to his own testimony, he delivered only two sermons from manuscript during his entire lifetime. He would have been glad to deliver more had his listeners been willing to tolerate the practice of having sermons read, but he advised younger preachers against it and, above all, warned them against burying their faces and their voices in a manuscript.

As a theologian, he was highly regarded in both English and German theological circles, and leading periodicals reviewed his publications. Impressive as they were for their learning and their many references to a wide variety of sources in several languages, ancient and modern, his books on theology nevertheless were heavy and uninspired and often dull.

It was at the editor's desk that he seemed most at home. As a German-trained scholar, he had a far better formal education than most of his contemporaries in the German Methodist church. His wide interests and his fund of knowledge covered many fields: history, politics, literature, and science, as well as theology. Early in his ministerial career, he became convinced that he had a sacred obligation to publish a journal in the German language which would not only serve as a vehicle for the dissemination of his religious faith, but also meet the demand for general news and information by recently arrived immigrants who needed to be Americanized and who would profit most from an American medium of communication published in their native German tongue.

James B. Finley, after a visit to Nast's editorial office in Cincinnati, reported that "his books, his papers, his assistant, and his very stove and table, all seem to be German," [1] and so they were, for Nast never ceased to think of himself as a German intellectual. But he was equally determined to develop a German-language paper which would both instruct his readers on religious matters and prepare them to be good citizens of their newly-adopted fatherland. He felt at home at the editor's desk and found journalism a congenial profession. He made *Der Christliche Apologete*, which he founded and edited for more than fifty years and which survived for more than a century, the leading German Methodist paper in the United States and a household necessity of many German Methodist homes. For fifty years, Nast was the *Apologete*, and the *Apologete* was Nast.

In 1828, the Western Methodist Book Concern was opened in Cincinnati as a branch of a New York company, and in 1836 it became an independent concern. The weekly *Western Christian Advocate* appeared in 1834; and in 1840 the *Ladies Repository and Gleanings of the West*, one of the first women's magazines in the United States, was launched by the Cincinnati Methodist publishing firm. Such publications were extremely important in the spread of Methodism, and it is not surprising that shortly after his conversion, Nast began to make plans for a Methodist paper which would appeal to his German constituency.

He received support for his project from a number of English-speaking Methodists. A Methodist minister in Waynesburg, Ohio, wrote to the *Christian Advocate* to urge the establishment of a German journal which would serve the German families in his circuit. He wanted it "freighted with Gospel truth, extracted from our standard works," and sent a contribution of ten dollars to help finance the project. Adam Miller wrote in a similar vein from Batavia, Ohio, and stressed the urgency of counteracting the pernicious influence of German infidels and Roman Catholics upon German Methodists. In another connection, Miller referred to Nast as "anointed for the office [of editor] as unexpectedly as David was elected to the throne." James B. Finley supported the project, and letters from several other prominent Methodists were printed in the *Western Christian Advocate*, whose editor, L. L. Hamline, had an abiding faith in the future of the German work.

Hamline presented the proposal for a German paper to the Methodist Conference in 1838, and in September of that year, the Ohio Conference officially authorized such a publication, with Nast as editor. There were some members of the Conference who believed "the infidel foreigners" were beyond redemption, and Nast tried to meet their objections by presenting a strong argument in the *Western Christian Advocate* in which he urged that every effort be made to rescue the German immigrant from "wicked and unreasonable men," before they quenched "the last strivings of the Holy Spirit." Nast was determined to save the Germans from infidels and freethinkers and from the "clerical pirates . . . under the flag of an orthodox Christian church" [Roman Catholic] who waged relentless warfare against the divided forces of Protestantism. According to him, a part of the German immigration was "held in the iron grasp of superstition, the other receiving the deadly drought of infidelity." [2] He was especially concerned about well-educated Germans who were eager to preserve German culture in America but opposed all organized religion, especially Methodism. [3]

A campaign for contributions of at least ten dollars from

each of three hundred donors, sponsored by the *Western Christian Advocate*, produced $1,500 within six months, and the first issue of the *Apologete*, whose original name was *Der Christliche Apologete und evangelischer Zuruf an die Deutschen von Amerika*, was dated January 4, 1839. The salutation of the editor was addressed "to our readers in the name of Jesus." Actually, copies of the paper had been circulated several weeks earlier in order to attract subscribers. In its original form, the *Apologete* was a four-page weekly, seventeen by eleven inches. The subscription rate was a dollar and a half a year, with a discount of twenty-five cents if subscribers paid within six months, and fifty cents if they paid in advance. Methodist ministers and circuit riders were authorized to act as solicitors and were expected to advertise the paper among their flocks.

Nast received a total of $2,400 from English-speaking Methodists and started the *Apologete* with about a hundred subscribers. By 1847, circulation had climbed to 1,700; by 1852, to double that number; and by 1855, to 6,175. In 1860, Nast pleaded for 10,000 subscribers, to commemorate the twenty-fifth anniversary "of his salvation in the blood of Jesus." By 1869, circulation reached 15,000. But even as late as 1850, the *Apologete* was running an annual deficit of $800.

Like other German-language papers, the *Apologete* always had a considerable number of delinquent subscribers. On one occasion, Nast paid for fifty subscriptions out of his own pocket for old readers who were too poor to renew, and a number of local preachers who could ill afford it, did likewise. The paper went to hospitals and prisons through special gifts. Preachers who collected delinquent accounts received a commission of 10 percent. From time to time, the publishers offered premiums, such as prints of John Wesley and the bishops, to stimulate circulation. In 1874, the *Apologete* had about 16,000 subscribers. The figure was encouraging but represented less than half the number of German Methodists in the United States at that time. In 1887, circulation passed the 18,000 mark, and the next year, the paper was enlarged to sixteen pages, of which two and a half were devoted to advertising. The high water mark in the history of the *Apologete* was reached in 1890, with 19,150. On December 3, 1941, 103 years after its founding, the last issue came from the press. By this time, the *Apologete* had shrunken to a monthly, and its subscriptions had dwindled to 3,000.

The *Apologete* was first of all " a defender of evangelical truth, a courageous representative of church interests, and a guide to conversion." Conversion of the individual received priority over questions of private and public morality, although the editor was by no means indifferent to such matters. The first number contained a diatribe against the Church of Rome, attacks on other so-called " dead " churches, and discussions of the sins and follies of unbelievers. It also contained articles on " neighborly love," Sunday schools, quotations from John Wesley, and essays on the wrath of God, original sin, salvation by faith, and the nature of Christ's mission of redemption. In his plea for support of his journal, Nast argued that the Germans were " a reading people," and that there were more of them in the Mississippi Valley than Indians beyond the Rockies, and " more Catholic, neologistic and skeptical Germans in this great west than there are heathens in the whole specific territory of the United States." He regarded the *Apologete* as one of the builders of Zion, and he thought it deserved as generous support as the missionary work of the Methodist church among the Indians. Moreover, it would become a bond of union among the widely scattered and expanding German missions, which soon covered the country from the Atlantic to California.

Despite his fervent appeals for help, circulation grew slowly. On one occasion, Peter Cartwright, the veteran circuit rider, sent him $10, and the New York mission contributed $120. By 1846, Nast could boast of a new, steam-driven press, and he eagerly looked forward to the day when he could extend the coverage of his paper to include general information and news from both America and Europe. In 1847, when he was offered a professorship at McKendree College in Illinois, he turned it down to remain in his editorial chair, despite the attractions which an academic post undoubtedly had for a scholar. In 1847, the size of the page of the *Apologete* was increased to twelve by seventeen inches, and in 1852, it was further enlarged to fourteen by nineteen.

With the January number of 1861, the *Apologete* became an eight-page weekly. Four pages were devoted entirely to religion, two to political and other news from the United States and abroad, and the last two to advertising, which was sold at the rate of a dollar for each ten lines. Nast referred to his paper as " the best advertising medium " for the Germans in the United States. To cover the cost of the larger edition, the price of subscriptions was raised a modest twenty-five cents a year.

Nast was overjoyed that at last he would be able to report and comment on daily news, without reducing the space given to religion. The issue of January 3, 1861, began volume XXIII and was the first to appear in the new format. The first page, as always, dealt exclusively with religious matters. The two pages devoted to general news were largely concerned with the developing crisis over secession but also carried foreign news items from Italy, Germany, France, Austria, Switzerland, China and Mexico. There was a short market report, and the paid advertising reflected the interests and habits of the foreign-born constituency which the paper served. There were advertisements from tobacconists, despite the church's attitude toward smoking; from physicians, life and fire insurance companies, dispensers of patent medicine remedies, sellers of hardware, furniture and other products; from a homeopathic pharmacist, publishers of religious books and distributors of ministers' and Sunday school supplies.

Nast had a number of assistant editors during his long reign as editor-in-chief. Some were men of real competence, but he alone determined the character of the *Apologete*. He was not without his severe critics, and in 1877, when he had to fight to retain the editorship, he received more support from the English-speaking delegates at the General Conference than from his German colleagues. Later, when he moved to Berea, Ohio, largely because of the insistence of his wife who wanted to get away from the dirt, smoke and heat of Cincinnati, criticism mounted, and many believed that the quality of the *Apologete* would deteriorate, with the editorial offices in Cincinnati and the editor living several hundred miles away. His salary, in 1880, was $2,500 plus $500 " for office help."

There were devoted readers of the *Apologete* who complained that it contained too many strange " high-toned" words, but Nast refused to apologize for his use of good German. On the other hand, there also were subscribers who pointed out that too many non-German expressions were creeping into the paper, for Nast, like most German immigrants, and despite his greater learning, succumbed to such Americanisms as " Främ Kirche," " Fenz," " Gerentet," " Retail

Preis" and other terms transferred phonetically from English into German. It was also somewhat disconcerting to the purists to find such expressions as "passierte folgende Beschlüsse," or "introducirt" the "minutes" of a conference.[4]

As he grew older, Nast reduced his own contributions to the *Apologete*, but he did not surrender any of his editorial prerogatives. In 1889, he agreed to confine his own contributions to articles dealing with Christian experiences and the exposition of Bible passages. He brought in his son Albert as his assistant and in 1892 had him elected as his successor at the Omaha General Conference. Of 471 votes cast, Albert received 365, demonstrating again that whenever the occasion demanded, Nast could be a master church politician.

The son quickly learned that the veteran senior editor had no intention of surrendering all control over policy matters. The Conference had given the elder Nast the title of "Honorary Editor," and as long as he was physically able and in residence in Cincinnati, Nast came to the office every day to exercise his proprietary interests. On several occasions, Albert accused his father of intolerance and pleaded for "some independence of thought," and there were occasional differences of opinion about what should be printed in the *Apologete*, but thanks to the deep affection between father and son, their differences never developed into serious conflicts.

The *Apologete* was the most influential German Methodist publication, and pious German Methodists eagerly looked forward to the arrival of this weekly visitor to their homes. But there were other Methodist publications in the German language, and before proceeding with a more detailed account of the *Apologete*'s religious character something should be said about its literary contemporaries.

Die Sonntagsschul-Glocke, founded in 1857, was designed for German Methodist Sunday schools. Three years later, it had a circulation of 14,000, and the total eventually reached 30,000. In 1871, *Der Bibelforscher*, also designed for Sunday school use, was started and at one time had a circulation of 44,000. In 1879, a four-page sheet, designed especially for children, entitled *Für kleine Leute* was published weekly and sold for $12 a hundred for the year. *Der Wegweiser zur Heiligung* was a monthly publication. The German Methodists also issued leaflets for juveniles, tracts, song-books, known by such titles as *Jugendharfe, Liederlust* and *Jubelklänge*, and other reading matter in the German language, totalling over 350 items. Heinrich Liebhart, who was assistant editor of the *Apologete* after 1865, helped develop a German "Youth Library" of a hundred titles. As a rival to Nast's Cincinnati paper, *Der evangelische Apologete* was published by Southern Methodists after the split in the church over slavery, and although it suspended publication during the Civil War, it was revived in New Orleans as a bi-weekly in 1868.

In 1873, *Haus und Herd* was established as a Christian family magazine. Under the able editorship of Liebhart, it developed into a first class illustrated monthly periodical, devoted to education, travel, poetry, history, science, and belles lettres, as well as church matters and miscellaneous subjects. Its contents were widely noted and reviewed in the German-language press, and such outstanding papers as the *Cincinnati Volksblatt*, the *Westliche Post* of St. Louis and the *Illinois Staatszeitung* of Chicago called the attention of their readers to the excellent reading material in *Haus und Herd*.

The *Apologete's* first service to its readers was to furnish them with reading material on religious subjects. Its files abound with discussions about the power of prayer, the experience of conversion, faith and salvation. The editor was profoundly interested in discovering whether conversion was spontaneous or came by stages, and how one attained salvation and what it really meant. This led him to critical examinations into the status of the soul after death, and before resurrection, and a discussion of what Jesus really looked like, and what kind of music was heard in heaven. On January 30, 1871, the *Apologete* carried an essay on "the art of dieing," and the most appropriate last words to be used on that final, solemn occasion; and for the sake of contrast, readers were frequently exposed to harrowing descriptions of the last hours of infidels like Tom Paine.

The *Apologete* reprinted sermons by bishops and others, the correspondence and transactions of church conferences, statistics about church membership, accounts of revivals and the activities of missionaries and circuit riders and the number of their converts. Nast also printed long expositions of Scriptural passages, and on the more practical side, discussed such issues as temperance and higher salaries for ministers.

As time went on, the *Apologete* gave less space to reports from individual pastors who longed for a little publicity and eagerly sent in accounts of what was going on in their churches. Readers complained that this material was uninteresting and repetitious. Nast also had to yield to a growing demand for more "entertainment literature." He readily agreed that church papers should be both readable and Christian, but he was particularly displeased with the wide circulation which Germany's *Gartenlaube* had among the Germans in America, for he regarded it as an infidel journal.

The long articles on theology which appeared regularly in the *Apologete*, and many of which Nast wrote himself, may have been feasts for scholars but hardly palatable daily fare for the average reader. Subscribers sometimes complained about the length of these theological disquisitions, but Nast replied that his paper was not primarily a journal of entertainment. He insisted that on questions of theology one must be thorough [5] and continued to publish dull and long-drawn-out, hair-splitting arguments over such topics as what was "complete salvation," "the baptism of the Holy Spirit," the exact nature of the sacraments, the precise meaning of the parables and the miracles, and just what it meant "to be born again." Among the parables, the tales of the prodigal son and the widow's mite seem to have been his special favorites. Occasionally, he dealt with such subjects as the creation, as revealed in geology and Holy Writ.[6]

The stories of individual conversions were many, and accounts of the deist whose Bible had been a deck of cards before he was brought to salvation and of the Catholic who turned Methodist were especially popular. Deathbed scenes were ideal material for vivid journalism, and no harrowing detail was overlooked. In the case of the believer, such scenes gave "foretastes of heaven"; in the case of agnostics, they portrayed the horror and fear of the damned. Material of this kind was sent to the *Apologete* by many readers and usually received a prominent place in the paper. Individual pastors sent in obituary notices of such length that Nast had to decline to print them all. Whenever he abridged them, he was severely criticised by both the family of the deceased and the pastor who had used the obituary notice as a vehicle for pulpit eloquence. Nast was also accused occasionally of refusing to publish contributions on theological matters unless the author's point of view coincided exactly with his own.[7]

The *Apologete* tried to give practical advice to ministers and congregations. In a series of articles in 1844, the editor undertook to enlighten his readers on the history of Methodism in the United States, and he reprinted sermons from which local ministers could draw both inspiration and models for their own preaching. The *Apologete* gave detailed accounts of the proceedings of Methodist conferences and reported the activities of many individual churches. In the issue of April 25, 1845, Nast discussed suggestions for family worship in the home. In 1863, he gave advice to ministers about to be transferred to other churches on how they could make the lot of their successors easier. The *Apologete* contained other advice about pulpit techniques, the selection of hymns, pastoral visits, class meetings and love feasts, intended to help beginners in the ministry. Occasionally Nast gave fatherly advice on how members should act toward their ministers. He published both his own sermons and translations of the work of such outstanding pulpit orators as Charles G. Finney of Oberlin and Henry Ward Beecher. The latter was one of Nast's special favorites until the Brooklyn preacher's reputation was blasted in the famous Tilton-Beecher adultery case. In general, Nast tried to avoid complicated philosophical questions in his preaching and in his quotations from others. He was convinced that the average churchgoer lacked the ability to follow such discussions, and he believed people were tired of Huxley, Tyndall, Spencer and Ingersoll and wanted to hear about Jesus.[8]

The *Apologete* also tried to provide reasonable coverage of the field of religious literature, and many issues carried announcements of new books on theology, science and religion, published in Germany as well as in this country. Many of these books could be had in the editorial office in Cincinnati. A leading reporter and reviewer of religious books was M. J. Cramer, who regularly sent reviews to the *Apologete* of books published on the Continent.

The *Apologete* is important also for the light it throws on the relation of German Methodism to other denominations, especially Lutherans and Catholics, who constituted the majority of the German immigration. It will be remembered that Nast himself had been baptized and confirmed in the Lutheran church and that he had prepared for a pastorate in that church at the University of Tübingen. His defection from the church of his native land did not make German Lutherans in America feel too kindly toward the Methodist renegade, and this may explain some of the sharp theological controversies in which German Methodists and Lutherans became involved in the United States. Whereas the Roman Catholic church paid little attention to Methodist attacks on Romanism and Papism, the Lutherans were persistently critical of their German brethren who had strayed into the Methodist fold, and the Missouri Lutheran Synod was especially hostile toward German Methodism. In 1847, for example, a series of articles in the *Apologete* precipitated a sharp controversy with Dr. C. F. W. Walther, "Lutheran Pope of the West," over communion, and in 1858, Walther ceased exchanging his *Lutheraner* for the *Apologete*.

From time to time, the *Apologete* also became involved in a battle of words with the *Lutherische Kirchenzeitung*, whose editor warned the Germans of the United States against the insidious propaganda of Methodist preachers. From the Lutheran viewpoint, Methodists were an uneducated lot, with little training in theology, who made up for their lack of preparation by noisy meetings and fanatical demonstrations of religious fervor which disturbed the peace of entire neighborhoods. The Methodist Discipline, which frowned upon most of the joys of life, and proscribed the dance, liquor, cards and the theater, proved especially unpalatable to German Lutherans who had the Continental notion about what were sinful pleasures.

In 1857, Nast locked horns with Dr. Philipp Schaff, distinguished Lutheran theologian, historian and pastor. Schaff had attacked Methodism in an article in his *Kirchenfreund*, published in Mercersburg, Pennsylvania, and the only German theological review in the United States. The purpose of the attack, repeated in Schaff's book, *The Political, Social and Ecclesiastical Condition of the United States*, was to redeem America "from the plague of sects." Ludwig Nippert replied to Schaff in the columns of the *Apologete*, but Nast published his counterattack in *The Methodist Quarterly Review*,[9] in order to reach the larger English-speaking Methodist membership, some of whom had sympathized with Schaff's criticisms of German Methodism. The exchange centered largely around the nature of German Methodist revivals and camp meetings. Schaff admitted that they might be "a salutary chastening rod for dead and sleepy preachers," but denounced the fanaticism, disorder and noise which accompanied such religious demonstrations. He referred to the "intellectual imbecility" of the German Methodists, to their "barbarous Christianity," and their perversion of a "God of order" into "a protector of disorder and fanaticism." Schaff also challenged the Methodist doctrine of the attainability of moral perfection in this life. He disposed of the *Apologete* "as a spiritless paper, full of unsalted piety and vain praisings of camp meetings and awakenings . . . radical in politics . . . ignoble and Jesuitical . . . unworthy of a Christian gentleman." Nast's reply to such unrestrained criticism was relatively mild. He characterized the charges as untrue and charged Schaff and his paper with having an evil animus toward all German Methodists.

Despite their deep-seated theological antagonisms, editors of German religious papers were especially alert to the practice of copying material from their columns without crediting the author. The *Apologete* accused the editors of Lutheran papers of numerous plagiarisms, and in 1859, Nast scolded the Mennonites for stealing material for their *Christliche Volksblatt*. In 1873, the *Apologete* was involved in a similar argument with the *Christliche Botschafter*, organ of the Evangelical Reformed church. The latter accused the *Apologete* of ten cases of plagiarism, and Nast retorted that the *Botschafter* had copied twice as many articles from his journal without indicating the source.

The controversy between Methodists and Catholics was long and acrimonious, and Nast and the *Apologete* engaged in it for many years, for in Nast's opinion, Roman Catholicism was not " Christian," either from the point of view of theology or church polity.

As early as 1844, the *Apologete* indulged in bitter exchanges with the *Wahrheitsfreund*, Cincinnati's German Catholic paper, which Nast once described as " a spider that sucks only poison from a flower." The editor of the *Wahrheitsfreund* was furious because Nast had reprinted from the New York *Schnellpost*, a German secular paper noted for its radicalism and anti-clericalism, articles about the growing power of the Jesuits in Germany and Switzerland. In a lead article of April 4, 1845, Nast explained the fundamental and irreconcilable differences between Protestantism and Catholicism. On other occasions, he made short shrift of the miracles claimed by the Catholic church, particularly in the area of miraculous cures from disease, and branded them as pure " humbug." [10]

In 1844, Nast published an article, " Catholicism in

America," which he took from the *Western Christian Advocate*. It attacked the growing political power of the Catholic priesthood, based primarily on the heavy Catholic immigration from Ireland and Germany. Catholics were charged with making a mockery of the Bible, destroying the public school system, and building up such political power that the " Pope could easily put a Polk or a Clay in the President's chair." [11] The *Apologete* looked hopefully for signs that might indicate the decline of Irish influence in the United States and deplored the intermarriage of Irish and Anglo-Americans. The woes of Ireland Nast attributed in large measure to the large sums of money sent from the Emerald Isle to fill the papal coffers in Rome; [12] and the backwardness of the Italians he attributed to the same pernicious influence of the church. In 1868, the *Apologete* printed a contribution from its perennial roving correspondent, M. J. Cramer, giving his impressions of a visit to Rome. The latter reported that he found little in Italy save " poverty, begging, ignorance, superstition and immorality," and a despotic church.[13]

On several occasions, the *Apologete* singled out John Hughes, the aggressive, fighting Catholic Archbishop of New York, for attack. During the Know-Nothing movement of the 1850's, which advocated restriction of immigration and was especially hostile to Irish Catholics, the *Apologete* agreed with the Cincinnati *Republikaner* that however extreme the methods and objectives of the nativists might be their real purpose was to clip the wings of the Roman Catholic hierarchy in the United States. In 1852, when a Roman Catholic priest debated with a Methodist in Portsmouth, Ohio, about the sacraments, both the *Apologete* and the Catholic *Wahrheitsfreund* furnished their readers with a detailed account of the encounter. According to the *Apologete*, Irish Catholics

were responsible in 1844 for the bloody nativist riots in Philadelphia which converted "a quiet city into a bloodbath."
Some twenty years later, when Orangemen rioted with Irish
Catholics in New York, the responsibility for the disorders
was again fixed upon the Catholics, and Nast quoted the
Baltimore *Wecker*, the *Westliche Post*, the *Anzeiger des
Westens* of St. Louis, and the *Illinois Staatszeitung* to support
his conclusions. Roman Catholic papers presented quite different versions of such deplorable incidents, and again and again,
the *Apologete* and the *Wahrheitsfreund* were involved in
bitter debate over nativism.

In 1875, Nast was seriously disturbed by rumors that
the Pope was about to come to America in order to escape
from his Vatican prison. He seized the occasion to point out
once more that, in his opinion, the whole concept of the
Papacy was a contradiction of that self-government and popular sovereignty on which the American republic was founded.[14]
When President Cleveland recognized the fiftieth anniversary
of the priesthood of Pope Leo XIII, by commissioning Archbishop Ryan of Philadelphia to give the Pope a specially
prepared copy of the American Constitution, the *Apologete*
repeated its contention that Catholicism and Americanism
were utterly incompatible.[15]

The battle over public versus parochial schools in which
Nast engaged a century ago remains a controversial issue in
parts of the nation even today. As far as the *Apologete* was
concerned, no compromise was possible. In Nast's mind, all
Catholics were enemies of public education. He gladly published the attacks of anti-Catholic agitators on the Catholic
parochial system, and in 1853, when the Catholics of Cincinnati asked for a share of public tax funds, Nast fought
vigorously with the *Catholic Telegraph* over the issue.

In periods of nativist agitation, America has several times been flooded with salacious, anti-Catholic articles dealing with alleged scandals among the priesthood and with what is reported to go on behind convent and monastery walls. Compared with some other editors of religious journals, Nast reprinted a minimum of such tales, but subscribers to the *Apologete* received their share of this kind of spicy reading. In 1844, for example, the *Apologete* reported the conviction of a priest in Evansville, Indiana, for raping a woman in the confessional.[16] Some years later, Nast printed the story of a nine-year-old girl whom the Catholics tried to force into a convent in Providence, Rhode Island,[17] and in the issue of November 6, 1856, the *Apologete* reported that a Catholic teacher in Cleveland beat an eight-year-old girl to death because she had attended a Protestant Sunday school. The financial difficulties of Archbishop Purcell of Cincinnati made less exciting reading but provided further grist for the *Apologete* for most of 1879. The paper reported the Archbishop's carelessness with several millions of other people's money which had been deposited with him for investment by faithful parishioners. 147582

Despite his consistently anti-Catholic attitude, Nast could, on occasion, speak with more charity about his theological enemies. When Archbishop Hughes died in 1864, the *Apologete* carried an obituary describing him as a talented leader of his church, a man of keen insight and much practical sense, cautious, yet always ready for battle. Nast believed the prelate's education had been neither broad nor deep, save in the highly specialized field of church history, but he regarded the archbishop as " a devoted, gifted and successful " leader of his church.[18] On another occasion, four years later, Nast gave "honor where honor is due," to Pope Pius IX, who helped a poor, aspiring Protestant artist to gain admission to the Academy of Rome and paid part of his fees.[19]

There was one Catholic journalist for whom Nast, like many other German editors of whatever political or religious persuasion, had genuine respect and even a measure of affection. This was Maximilian Oertel, editor of the *Katholische Kirchenzeitung* of New York. Pater Oertel, as he was widely known, was a unique figure in the field of German-American journalism. Trained in a German university as an "old Lutheran," Oertel came to the United States in 1837 and preached in several eastern pulpits before he was converted to Catholicism in 1840. He served on the faculty of several Catholic institutions. He was a man of great learning, a devout and genial Catholic, unusually tolerant, a good journalist, a roguish and often coarse humorist, a lover of wine and the jolly company of friends of all religious and political faiths, with whom he met regularly in the taverns. Much of his writing was in verse form. He crossed swords with freethinkers like Karl Heinzen and Friedrich Hassaurek, with C. F. Walther of the Missouri Lutherans, and with Nast of the Methodists, but somehow he managed to keep the respect of most of his adversaries, who recognized in him a genial, brilliant foeman worthy of their steel. Oertel read the *Apologete* and Nast read his *Katholische Kirchenzeitung*. In one issue, Oertel maintained that the Methodist doctrine of salvation and good works was like that of the Catholics, and in 1878, Nast wrote a warm congratulatory message on the occasion of the twenty-eighth anniversary of Oertel's journal.

As far as the Jewish faith was concerned, the attitude of the *Apologete* cannot be so clearly defined as its attitude toward the Catholics. Moreover, there was considerable difference of opinion between Nast's own views and those of several contributors who wrote on the question. A number

of articles in the *Apologete* reflected the anti-Semitic senti-
ment that was spreading among certain groups in Germany,
and Ludwig Nippert's reports to the *Apologete* from West-
phalia frequently struck an anti-Semitic note.[20] Other corre-
spondents belabored the growing economic power of the Jews
of Germany. Nast found space for unfavorable characteri-
zations of the Jews but argued that only by spreading Christianity among them could the undesirable traits of the Jewish
people be eradicated. He condemned the pogroms in Romania
and urged the United States government to intervene to
protect the Jews from further outrages. The *Apologete* was
more tolerant toward Jews while Nast was its editor than
during the later years when the paper was managed by
his son. The latter's regime was marked by a stronger over-
tone of anti-Semitism, and in a number of issues, the *Apologete* carried little tales for juveniles which, while not vicious,
held up the Jews to ridicule as clever, shrewd, not too scrupu-
lous operators, primarily interested in sharp business deals
(" Zu mache a G'schäftele ").[21]

The elder Nast's solution for the Jewish question was
naively simple—do more missionary work among them and
convert them to Methodism! " Ordinarily," he wrote in the
issue of January 5, 1888, " one passes by the Jew, as though
he had no soul." A week later, he specifically denounced the
growing anti-Semitism here and abroad. He was deeply interested in a Methodist mission for Jews established in Galena,
Illinois, and he was delighted when a missionary paper, known
as the *Immanuel*, was distributed free among Methodist and
other ministers to stimulate them to convert Jews to Christianity.[22]

Lutherans, Catholics and Jews received major attention
in the *Apologete*, but other denominations were not totally
ignored. Unitarians obviously were beyond the pale, for they

denied the divinity of Jesus and salvation by his blood. According to Nast, he who does not have the Son cannot have the Father either. It is not without interest, however, to find that when Nast died one of the warmest tributes to his career appeared in a Unitarian journal, which referred to him as "the German Wesley" and compared him with Count Zinzendorf of the Moravians. The obituary stressed Nast's simple piety and devotion and his reputation as a Biblical scholar.[23]

The Universalists Nast classified with the Catholics, and maintained that both paved the way to atheism, although he regarded Universalism as the more dangerous.[24] Felix Adler's new liberal religion of "practical justice and social service," which blossomed into the Ethical Culture societies, Nast predicted would fail because it sought to achieve its ends without the help that must come from God and the spirit of Christ. Nast recognized Robert G. Ingersoll, "the Goliath of infidelity," as an orator without equal and reprinted in the *Apologete* part of his oration at the grave of his brother but considered Ingersoll's whole career as proof of the bankruptcy and hopelessness of atheism.

While Nast was still in the editor's chair, he also published a number of sharp attacks on Christian Science. A Methodist colleague, George L. Mulfinger, contributed several articles in 1858, which likened Emanuel Swedenborg to such misguided religious leaders as Mohammed and Joseph Smith and argued that Swedenborgianism was at variance with many of the truths of Christianity. Nast was more charitable, and in 1869, wrote an editorial tribute to Swedenborg. Such groups as the Millerites, who predicted the end of the world in 1844, he dismissed as unbalanced fanatics. And he considered spiritualists and fortune tellers in the same category and advised his readers to shun them.

8

THE *APOLOGETE* AS A JOURNAL OF
NEWS AND INFORMATION

$\mathfrak{B}$esides saving souls by the processes of German Methodism, Nast wanted to Americanize his fellow German immigrants and make them good, well-adjusted citizens of the United States. As a scholar and an avid reader, he wanted to furnish reliable news and sound information on subjects other than religion to the readers of his *Apologete*. From the beginning, he had inserted items of general information, but in January 1861, he was able to expand his publication to include an entire section devoted to public affairs and secular matters. For a time the supplement was published separately and known as the *weltliche Beilage* (worldly supplement). A discussion of the *Apologete* as a news journal is in many ways as important as a study of its religious content, for the files throw light on what Nast considered important in the realm of public affairs and on his own views on important issues. They also reflect the experiences of German immigrant communities.

Like other newspapers, the *Apologete* reported fires, floods, steamship disasters and other events of everyday interest to the general reader. Nast was equally interested, however, in intellectual and cultural matters, from long book reviews to accounts of the Cincinnati May Festival and biographical essays of outstanding historical figures, such as Ulrich von Hutten, Ulrich Zwingli, and others drawn both from religious and secular history. He was also interested in travel accounts. In 1868, for example, the *Apologete* reviewed and reprinted large parts of Friedrich Hassaurek's *Four Years Among Spanish-Americans*, a volume by a fellow Cincinnatian based on the author's observations while serving as United States minister to Ecuador.

Nast always had great interest in medical questions. Something of a hypochondriac himself, he believed that such material would be of special interest to immigrant readers who were still prevented, by language barriers, from using the medical facilities available to Americans generally. The immigrant press of all nationality groups is striking evidence of the extent to which its readers have been the prey of patent medicines and the slaves of folk superstitions. Nast accepted all kinds of medical advertisements for the *Apologete*, and occasionally wrote personal endorsements of specific remedies, which were supposed to effect miraculous cures.

In its earliest issues, the *Apologete* advertised cures for the afflictions of both men and beasts, especially farm animals. For human beings, popcorn was supposed to cure diarrhoea, and charcoal, to improve the teeth and breath. For a " cold fever," the *Apologete* prescribed a fresh egg, soaked in red wine, the potion to be drunk " on the first feeling of the chill," and the dose to be repeated as often as necessary, presumably depending on the effect the alcoholic content would have on the patient.[1] A minister writing from Indiana recommended cod-liver oil, charcoal and warm milk as a cure for tuberculosis. On one occasion, Nast himself endorsed a cure for tuberculosis, concocted by a Cincinnati doctor, to be inhaled, rather than taken into the body by way of mouth and stomach.[2] One finds advertisements for "patent cornea restorers" to cure blindness; for painless dentistry; for cough, headache and cancer cures; for Dr. Scott's Electric Plasters, with a pair of electric insoles free to the buyer; for Ayer's Hair Vigor to combat gray hair; for Wagner's Fever Drops, personally endorsed by Nast; for Scovill's Blood and Liver Syrup; for Ayer's Cherry Pectoral, another concoction with a strong alcohol base, for respiratory troubles; for Pierce's Pleasant Purgative Pellets; for Sapanule to cure skin diseases by absorption; and for the famous old German remedy, *St. Jakob's Oel*, made from needles of cedar trees in the Black Forest and good for almost everything.

In the spring of 1860, the *Apologete* began a series of articles on the human body, which was a strange mixture of religion and medicine, but which undertook to explain some of the basic facts of anatomy and physiology and the causes of disease. Occasionally, the paper carried discussions of scientific subjects. In 1875, Nast finally felt the time had come to warn his readers that they took patent medicines advertised in his paper at their own risk. He went on to explain that he himself followed the homeopathic school of medicine and that some patent medicines advertised in his paper he would not take even if he got them free. Nevertheless, he maintained that in a free country like the United States no editor or publisher could control advertising. The

Apologete was particularly helpful in advertising products sold by superannuated ministers to supplement their pitifully low incomes. In 1859, for example, a retired German Methodist minister from Belleville, Illinois, offered for twelve dollars a kit of 104 homeopathic remedies along with a doctor's book to enable anyone to diagnose his ills and treat himself.[3]

The *Apologete* also was interested in serving the farmers and housewives who constituted a large proportion of its readers. Nast published advice on many subjects, from recipes for cooking to how to keep fence posts (*Fenz-Posten*) from rotting.[4] The *Apologete* printed directions for building cisterns and keeping them sanitary; for planting and harvesting various crops; for treating diseased cattle; and for best methods and the proper time for pruning trees. In the issue of September 30, 1858, it quoted from the *American Agriculturist* on waterproof cement. In a day of fluctuating values of bank notes and currency, it also printed market reports from the leading trading centers of the United States, warnings about counterfeit money, discount rates for bank paper, and the exchange ratio for European currencies.

The paid advertising of the *Apologete* called attention to almost everything in common use, from copper lightning rods, agricultural implements, gas lamps, life and fire insurance, piano melodeons and organs, to Ivory soap ("which floats like a cork") and Gold Dust Washing Powder, which enabled women "to get through work as early as their husbands." Advertisements by publishers and authors included many works on Methodism and religion but also special publications for farmers, stock and poultry raisers, and homeopathic physicians; exposés of the Masons and Odd Fellows; a juvenile Sunday school library with such intriguing titles as *Little Mabel and her Sunlit Home* and *What Catherine Did, and*

What Came of It; a handbook of arithmetic, in German; and aids to the study of English.

Like other immigrant papers, the *Apologete* served as an information office for missing persons. The March 8, 1844, issue, for example, carried a notice, "Where is Adolf König?" gave the town in Germany from which he had emigrated, and added that "two years ago he was working on the Miami Canal. . . ." Fathers inquired about missing sons, sisters for their brothers, and friends for friends, and expected the columns of the *Apologete* to help them reestablish contact with the missing persons.

The *Apologete* also carried frequent appeals for relief and financial aid. An Indiana farmer, whose smokehouse had burned down with a thousand pounds of meat, announced that he was a good Methodist and appealed to fellow religionists for donations to help him weather his financial crisis.[5] An Ohio circuit rider lost his horse and asked for contributions so that he could buy another. A minister in Iowa paid a substitute $650 to escape being drafted during the Civil War, and requested readers of the *Apologete* to help him raise the amount, since his own congregation numbered only forty-two members. On another occasion, a minister asked for $150 to procure a cork leg for a parishioner who had been crushed under a load of coal. In 1855, a childless couple used the *Apologete* to advertise their desire to adopt a boy and girl.

Nast exercised his editorial office to tell parents how to rear their children, and many of his comments were strikingly progressive and modern. In 1844, in a series of articles drawn largely from the *Christliche Zeitschrift*, he urged that children be taught to respect property rights, that they not be pushed too fast by parents, and that the learning process be made more gradual and attractive, based on developing a child's interests and love for the subject. In 1868, he wrote a pedagogical essay pleading with parents to respect the rights of their children and admonishing them to refrain from criticism and iron discipline, especially during the period of adolescence. In the later years of his editorship, the *Apologete* carried a " children's column," heavily weighted with religious material and pleas to take the temperance pledge, but Nast made an honest attempt to make the paper interesting to juveniles. Occasionally, little serial stories were included as " dessert " for the readers, some of whom promptly complained that the selections contained no love story. In his time the pseudoscience of phrenology enjoyed wide popularity, and many believed it offered the clue by which pedagogues could develop desirable qualities of mind and conduct in their pupils, but he denounced the phrenological charts of his day as utterly unreliable for character analysis.

Like most foreign-language papers, the *Apologete* also published original poems, which flowed into the editor's office in such volume that he had to explain that he could not find room for them all and that many of these poetic effusions were marked by both bad grammar and bad rhyming, which he had neither the talent nor the time to revise for publication. He urged contributors to learn to write good prose before turning to poetry; needless to say, he offended many readers with his rejection slips.

Perhaps the first major public issue to confront the nation after Nast assumed the editorship of the *Apologete* was the Mexican War, which many Northerners opposed as a conspiracy of an aggressive slavocracy to acquire more territory for the expansion of the slave system at the expense of a weak southern neighbor. Nast manifested little interest in the moral issue involved. He followed the progress of the war with considerable enthusiasm, celebrated General Taylor's victory at Buena Vista and General Scott's at Vera Cruz and Mexico City but revealed little understanding of the sectional controversy that was bound to follow the annexation of Mexican territory at the end of the war. The nearest approach to a discussion of fundamental issues is found in the issue of November 27, 1845, in which Nast translated an article from the *Christian Advocate and Journal*, whose main thesis was that war, like cholera, was a scourge that had to be borne, but that the Lord might have in mind the overthrow of the power of the Roman priesthood in Mexico and had selected the United States army as the instrument to establish civil and religious liberty in a backward country.

Slavery was another matter. Although John Wesley had condemned it as " the execrable sum of all villanies," the Ohio Methodist Conference of 1835 vigorously denounced the propaganda of the abolitionists, and in 1844, the Methodist church split over the slavery question into a Northern and Southern church. Nast followed the growing controversy in the *Apologete*, and appealed to the Germans in particular to help rid the country of the curse of human bondage. He argued that since immigrants had come to the United States to escape oppression and obtain liberty and equality, they could not consistently defend holding any one in chains. As the sectional controversy developed, he became a strong antislavery man, who courageously voted his convictions in the General Conferences which he attended, although some of the bishops pleaded with the German delegations not to widen the breach between North and South. Because of his strong anti-slavery position, he became temporarily unpopular in church circles in Kentucky and decided to transfer his residence from Covington across the river to Cincinnati.

During the 1850's, the *Apologete* chronicled the gory details of "bleeding Kansas," and the bitter civil war in progress in that territory. Nast attended anti-Nebraska meetings, denounced the fugitive slave law of 1850 and the Dred Scott decision, and demanded the extinction of the South's peculiar institution.[6] In a lead article on August 7, 1856, entitled "The Christian in the Voting Booth," he implored his readers to seek divine aid before they cast their ballots but insisted that no one could remain neutral on the slavery question. He believed it was not the function of ministers to dictate to their parishioners on how to vote, but he urged a careful study of the issues by each congregation. The final solution, he believed, would not be found in the arena of politics, but in the regeneration of the human race through a more vigorous preaching of the Gospel.

As late as 1861, a gathering of German Methodist ministers adopted ambiguous resolutions condemning slavery when practiced "for mercenary reasons," but not under all circumstances, and some of the delegates from Kentucky objected when Nast supported even so mild a statement. On June 23, 1862, the *Apologete* demanded emancipation for all slaves, for "slavery has besmirched our morality, diplomacy, our homes and our foreign policy." In later issues, Nast advocated equal rights for the Negro, and after the war, he condemned discriminations based on color, not only in the South, but in Northern restaurants and at West Point as well.

As the irrepressible conflict over slavery moved into actual warfare, German Methodism divided, like other denominations, along sectional lines. The *Evangelische Apologete*, the Southern rival of Nast's Cincinnati publication, denounced

John Brown as a robber, murderer and arsonist, and defended the Southern viewpoint on the sectional crisis. As the gap between Southern and Northern German Methodists widened, Nast gave more space to the controversy. In the fall of 1860, a local postmaster in Texas refused to deliver the *Apologete* on the ground that it was an incendiary publication. Nast offered to send Southern readers only the religious portion of his paper, but he protested vigorously to the postmaster general against violations of freedom of speech and freedom of the mails in the Southern states. Nast certainly was not an extremist. On occasion, he denounced both abolitionists and Southern fire-eaters for driving the nation into war. He believed that the great majority of Americans wanted to avoid the dissolution of the Union, but he was sure that secession would end slavery throughout the United States.[7]

When the shooting began at Fort Sumter, the issues, as far as the *Apologete* was concerned, were quite clear. On one side were justice and liberty, on the other, slavery and treason. Nast concluded that the war was "providential," and that therefore Americans must be prepared to pay whatever price heaven demanded for the preservation of the Constitution, the Union and liberty.[8] Nast promptly printed a German translation of "The Star Spangled Banner," along with a plea for prayer and fasting by all the faithful.

The German element made a distinguished record in the Civil War. The *Apologete* carried a number of appeals for volunteers. One came from Nast's cousin, who claimed to have had fourteen years of military experience abroad and had obtained a lieutenant's commission; another was from a Chicagoan who had been authorized to raise four companies of cavalry, and wanted "soldiers who pray" and "who have faith in God as the Lord of Battles."[9] A hundred employees of the Methodist Book Concern in Cincinnati staged a patriotic demonstration on the roof of their building, raised a fifty-foot flag pole, fired salutes to the Union, and listened to prayers and exhortations from several Methodist ministers.[10] Copies of the *Apologete* were sent to volunteers in the army camps. Nast also had cancellations from readers who resented his strong endorsement of the Lincoln administration.

In August 1864, at the first meeting of the Central German Methodist Conference, which assembled in Nast's church on Race Street, resolutions were adopted endorsing Lincoln, condemning rebellion as a sin against God and country, and insisting that the war must continue until the last slave was free. The Conference appealed to the Germans to do their " holiest duty " for " our beloved adopted fatherland " and pointed with pride to the number of German Methodists (" our branch of Zion ") who were serving in the Union Army. Nast had the honor of transmitting these resolutions to the White House. Among his most treasured possessions was the letter he received from Lincoln, dated October 31, 1864, in which the President expressed his appreciation and added, " The conduct of your people since the outbreak of this desolating rebellion has been the best proof of the sincerity of your present professions."

The *Apologete* covered the war in both its military and political aspects as well as most German-language papers did, and better than some. It provided its readers with translations of all important government documents and Presidential messages. Nast himself translated Lincoln's first inaugural into beautiful German, and hailed the message as a " loving, conciliatory and peace-loving " appeal. The *Apologete* explained various congressional enactments, such as the draft and tax laws and thus demonstrated once more the important role which the foreign-language press has to perform in times of crisis for people who have not yet mastered English. In 1863, Nast published his German version of Lincoln's and Everett's addresses at Gettysburg.[11] The *Apologete* also carried many letters from soldiers at the front.[12]

The record of the foreign-born in the Civil War was a complete refutation of the charges of nativists who had questioned the loyalty of America's adopted citizens in the 1850's. There were hundreds of German names on the muster roll of the Union Army, and many Germans had commissions and military titles and wore gold braid. The Civil War had its full quota of political generals, but the German-language press insisted that Germans did not get their proper share of officers, and that those who received commissions suffered from the prejudices of the nativists and the professional West Pointers. On several occasions during the war, the controversy between native and foreign-born became sharp and bitter. It focussed largely on the careers of such German officers as Carl Schurz and Franz Sigel. Schurz was clearly a political general; Sigel had been an officer in the German Revolution of 1848-49. Schurz commanded a division of the Eleventh Corps which was decisively beaten at Chancellorsville. Thereafter the *New York Times* referred sarcastically to the " flying Dutchmen." Sigel had resigned his commission in Missouri after an encounter with General Halleck and had demanded an independent command.

Practically the entire German-language press became involved in the bitter argument over the merits and just deserts of Schurz and Sigel. We need not follow the exchanges with the nativist press in detail,[13] but it is interesting to point out that the *Apologete* was as vigorous in its defence of the Germans as any secular paper. As a German, Nast was jealous of the reputation of his countrymen. He quoted leading German papers to disprove the charges of cowardice against Schurz and his German division, and he maintained that Sigel was the victim of jealous and stupid West Pointers and deserved a major command.

In April 1865, Lincoln was felled by the bullet of an assassin. The *Apologete* carried a long editorial by Nast entitled, "The Nation in Mourning," which restated his unwavering belief that whatever happens must be according to a divine plan. He contended that God, in His infinite wisdom, had permitted Lincoln's assassination at the precise moment when the nation's prayers of thanksgiving for his leadership were mounting to heaven. Moreover, God had allowed the war to continue until the slaves were freed, and the martyrdom of the President was part of a plan to make Lincoln an even greater force in the life of the nation than he would have been if he had been permitted to serve out his second term. Nast thought Booth's crime would convince both North and South of the iniquity of rebellion and bring about genuine repentance. He observed that God's ways are not man's ways and closed his tribute to Lincoln with an appeal to the faithful to pray for Andrew Johnson, on whose shoulders the heavy burden of reuniting the nation had fallen.[14]

At the close of the war, Northern Methodism made a serious effort to replace the influence of the Methodist Church South with a reunited church, controlled from the North. Extensive missionary work was begun among the freedmen, and the Methodist Church North inevitably became identified with the plan of reconstruction sponsored by Republican radicals, for the success of its church program would depend largely on the success of congressional reconstruction. As a matter of fact, Southerners resented Methodist missionaries from the North; Negroes organized their own African Methodist church; and in the mounting bitterness over the racial question, Southern Methodists became even more determined to retain their sectional church organization.[15]

Nast supported the congressional plan of reconstruction rather than the milder programs of Lincoln and Johnson. He favored the Fourteenth Amendment and fundamental changes in the Southern economic and social system, which he believed only Congress could make. As time went on, however, and confusion, corruption and social strife continued in the Southern states, the *Apologete* took a more conservative position, although it continued to denounce such organizations as the Ku Klux Klan. When Johnson died in 1875, Nast wrote an editorial tribute to a man whom he had often attacked while in office, lauding him for his " courage, some political insight and unimpeachable honesty." [16]

After the Civil War, the *Apologete* continued to comment on national politics, to the displeasure of some readers who believed the paper was either too radical or too conservative and, in any case, should give its attention solely to religion. Nast continued to translate important messages and addresses by Presidents and governors, and to summarize important legislation. A staunch Republican, he endorsed General Grant in 1868 without actually mentioning his name as a sound-money man and a civil-service reformer. Like many others, he argued that the country must not be surrendered to the party of rebellion, especially since Roman Catholics played such a prominent role in the Democratic organization.

In 1872, many prominent German-Americans deserted Grant to help form the Liberal Republican party, whose candidate, Horace Greeley, became the standard-bearer of the Democratic party also. Nast remained faithful to Grant and expressed his admiration for his "modest patriotism, firmness of conviction, healthy judgment, practical wisdom, incorruptible honesty and distinguished services." [17] The *Apologete* forecast that Greeley and the Democratic party would prove about as compatible as fire and water. [18]

Like many others, Nast was disillusioned by the many scandals that came to light during Grant's second term, yet he continued to praise the general as a sound-money man, who was never misled by either the Greenbackers or the crusaders for Free Silver. In 1876, the *Apologete* was sympathetic with the Independents and was satisfied with the choice of Rutherford B. Hayes in the famous disputed election of that year. In 1875, Nast opposed a movement by churchmen to secure a Constitutional amendment proclaiming God, Jesus and the Bible as the foundation stones of the American republic, for he believed such a pronouncement could have no practical effect and might clear the way for a union of church and state, the curse of several European nations. [19] In the national campaign of 1880, the *Apologete* expressed no preference between Hancock and Garfield and endorsed both as good Christians uncontrolled by political machines. Nast was quite a little disturbed, however, when he found Ingersoll and Beecher speaking from the same platform on behalf of Garfield and making complimentary references to each other. [20]

Nast never advocated the social gospel, in any modern sense, and always insisted on individual conversion as the best way to build a Christian society. Nevertheless, he could not entirely ignore the developing struggle between capital and labor, which in the last quarter of the century resulted in several crises that seemed to foreshadow a social revolution. He sympathized with the laboring class and was eager to improve their lot. On several occasions, his paper described the pitiful condition of the " factory slaves," their long hours, poor wages, the wastefulness of strikes, and the exploitation of employees at company stores. He saw the need for sweeping changes, yet shrank from extreme remedies, and continued to argue that in the principles of Jesus the solution for the problems of modern industrial society could be found. He advised workingmen to proceed " through the quiet and noble Christian way of life " by the application of the Golden Rule, and he gave similar advice to their capitalist employers.[21] During his early years in America, he had commented favorably upon socialism and communism, as roads to reform, but later he came to regard them as destructive of organized society.

The *Apologete* insisted that the Christian church was not indifferent to the condition of the laboring man but that all schemes for reform would fail unless society could be reconstructed along Christian principles and geared to the ideal of the greatest happiness for the greatest number. Nast favored free homesteads for actual settlers and a government supported plan of internal improvements. In 1872, when the demand for an eight-hour day resulted in rioting in New York, he became profoundly disturbed and denounced the eight-hour movement as a swindle by which labor was being exploited by drones and demagogues. He was afraid that workers would misuse their leisure rather than devote their spare time to " intellectual and spiritual development, or to improve their homes." [22] He expressed the prevailing laissez-faire doctrines by opposing all " protective legislation " except in cases where it could be clearly demonstrated that the consumer was being gouged by an artificially inflated price level.[23] He opposed strikes as wasteful and thought that many of them "are worked out in saloons and . . . are especially profitable for saloons." He thought more favorably of the Knights of Labor, because their Grand Master Workman, Terence V. Powderly, was a temperance man. He deplored the unrestricted immigration of Polish Jews, affected with anarchism and atheism, and proposed sending more Christian missionaries to work among the Jews. On some of these matters, the *Apologete* became even more conservative after Nast's retirement from the editorship. Though the paper was sympathetic toward tax reforms, co-operatives, government control of railroads, and better educational facilities, it would have no traffic with Socialism because of its alleged anti-Christian attitude.[24]

Nast attributed the labor riots of 1877, in Pittsburgh and elsewhere, to the evil influence of "communism." The panaceas of Greenbackers and Free Silverites he rejected unequivocally as unsound. He viewed the rapid rise of the Social Democratic party in Germany with alarm. In 1894, when the *Apologete* was no longer in his control, it denounced Governor Altgeld of Illinois for pardoning the anarchists convicted in connection with the Haymarket Riot in Chicago and criticised the American Federation of Labor for its failure to rid its ranks of anarchists and socialists.[25]

Equal rights for women were almost unanimously denounced in the German-language press, which insisted that woman's place was in the home and with the family. A few radicals, like Karl Heinzen, crusaded for women's rights, but theirs were feeble voices raised against a storm of opposition. Nast did not approve of the extreme views published year after year in Heinzen's *Pionier*. On the other hand, he disagreed on this issue with many of his German fellow editors and churchmen. In 1854, in a statement of his position published in the *Apologete*, he advocated giving married women full rights to their property and favored the right of widows to be the legal guardians of their children. He wanted all legal barriers to equality, including the right to vote, removed on the simple American principle that there should be no taxation without representation.[26] He was ahead of his time on this issue. As late as 1890, the *Apologete* was still debating whether women should be accepted as delegates to Methodist conferences.

9

A BRIDGE BETWEEN TWO
CONTINENTS

The editor of an American paper published in a foreign language for a particular immigrant group must keep his eyes fixed on both sides of the Atlantic. He frequently finds himself looking backward and forward at the same time, for his readers are interested in what is going on both in the new land of their choice and in the old fatherland as well. Memories linger long, and the eyes of the immigrant turn often, with longing and nostalgia, to a homeland to which he has said a final farewell. Only time and new experiences will eventually settle the problem of how to make the proper blend between the old and the new. Thus, the immigrant press must help its readers preserve, as long as possible, the cultural heritage of the land of their origin, and at the same time guide them to a harmonious adjustment to new experiences in the land of their adoption. The immigrant press of the United States has been the most effective instrument for preserving the natural emotional ties between the old country and the new, during the newcomer's early years of residence in America, and for developing a process of Americanization with a minimum of maladjustments or emotional crises.[1]

Nast, as editor of the *Apologete*, understood these responsibilities. As a cultured gentleman scholar, his intellectual ties with Germany remained unbroken. He tried to keep his readers informed of major developments in the fatherland, particularly in the political and intellectual fields, and he did not hesitate to offer his own interpretations of events, as he saw them through the eyes of one who had become quickly Americanized.

From its beginning, the *Apologete* carried foreign news from all the major European countries, and to a lesser degree, from China and the Orient as well. In the issue of March 29, 1844, for example, one finds a review of the political situation in each of the leading countries of Europe. Nast's comments were generally slanted from the viewpoint of a minister of a Christian church, and whenever possible they referred to the struggle between Protestants and Catholics, but they showed an amazing familiarity with European affairs as a whole. In 1846, for example, the *Apologete* reported Sir Robert Peel's views on free trade and presented a clear statement of what this change in British policy would mean to the world. In 1858, Nast hailed the completion of the Atlantic cable as a major step toward world understanding, and the triumph of truth and justice. The first woodcut ever printed in the *Apologete* was an illustration of how the cable was constructed.[2]

Nast was keenly interested in Cavour's plans for the unification of Italy, and hoped their success would mean the collapse of the Papacy. The *Apologete* carried articles dealing with revolutionary ferment in Russia and with Garibaldi and the Republicans of Italy. It explained the significance of the Parliamentary Reform Bill of 1867 for the British people. It denounced the Fenian movement by American Irishmen, to twist the tail of the British lion by invading Canada, as a foolhardy tragi-comedy, which clearly violated American neutrality laws. During the Russo-Turkish War, the *Apologete*, on May 21, 1877, provided its readers with a full page map of Turkey and Asia Minor.

These are but samples of the *Apologete's* coverage of general European news. Obviously, events in the German fatherland were of greater interest to American German Methodists than what was going on in other parts of the world. When revolution broke out in 1848 in many of the German states, the German-language press in the United States followed its progress with enthusiasm and great expectations and provided its readers with a detailed account of the progress of the uprising against monarchical authority and the vestiges of feudalism. The German revolution of 1848 marked the belated sproutings of seeds sown by the French Revolution and scattered over Europe during the age of Napoleon. It found many of its leaders among the intellectuals, who were the product of the European Enlightenment and who wanted to unify Germany under a republican form of government. The cosmopolitan humanitarianism of these leaders was based on noble concepts of natural law and the rights of man, and the Frankfurt Parliament, the sounding board for such concepts, contained many university men who were motivated by high ideals and deep moral convictions.

Unfortunately for Germany and the world, the revolution failed. History had arrived at a turning point but failed to turn, and Germany sank back into a period of division and tyranny and was finally united in 1871 by methods quite different from those of the dreamers of 1848. Some ten thousand political refugees of the revolution fled to Switzerland, France and England, and many finally reached the United States. The great migration of the early 1850's brought many uprooted intellectuals to America, who were steeped in the culture and spirit of Kant, Fichte and Schiller. They came in sufficient numbers to provide a leadership for America's German element which was unique in the history of American immigration and which inaugurated the " Hellenic Age " of German culture in the United States. Among the newcomers were irrepressible romantics like Friedrich Hecker; ardent, combative and impractical world reformers like Karl Heinzen and Wilhelm Weitling; young radicals like Friedrich Hassaurek of Cincinnati; journalists like Friedrich Kapp and Oswald Ottendörfer of New York, August Thieme of Cleveland and Bernhard Domschke of Milwaukee; pedagogues like Adolf Douai and Friedrich Knapp, to whom Henry L. Mencken went to school in Baltimore; poets like Konrad Krez; able lawyers; doctors like Abraham Jacobi of New York and Hermann Kiefer of Detroit; and many others, including Carl Schurz, perhaps the greatest of the " Forty-Eighters." [3]

In contrast with the German-language press as a whole, Nast's *Apologete* paid relatively little attention to the revolution of 1848 but a great deal to the radicals and freethinkers among the political refugees whom the revolution disgorged on American shores. In the general category of freethinkers belonged all those who fought clericalism, dogmatism and supernaturalism, who rejected faith in a personal God, and who wanted to substitute a new rationalism for what they called an age of superstition. Among them were deists, agnostics, atheists, pantheists and humanists, and out-and-out materialists. In the eyes of the church people no fine distinctions should be made among them; they were all infidels and atheists. In America, they fought Puritanism, all forms of theology and the Catholic church in particular. In addition, they battled against an American Sabbatarianism which, in their opinion, had reduced Sunday to " a day of gloom " and " the rest of the tomb." For most Germans, Sunday was a day for dances, picnics, parades, dramatic performances, athletic demonstrations, music and beer gardens; and, in their arguments in favor of the " Continental Sunday," the Germans were as intolerant of American church people as the latter were of them. To the freethinkers, the Sabbatarians were " barbarians and Methodists."

It is apparent from the files of the *Apologete* that Nast was far more concerned with the consequences of the revolution for America than for Germany. He looked with alarm upon the migration of German freethinkers to the United States in the early 1850's, and opposed their efforts to spread what he considered the poison of rationalism, agnosticism and materialism among the German masses. There could hardly have been a wider cleavage than the one which developed between German Methodists and the radical refugees of 1848, whose views were diametrically opposed to the rule of conduct prescribed in the Methodist Discipline. Still worse, in Nast's opinion, the refugees were the enemies of all evangelical religions. Nast took up the cudgels against infidels and atheists in order to save his fellow German-Americans from the virus of an imported rationalism. When he considered the whole problem of Americanizing the immigrant, the religious motivation always was uppermost in his mind. As it turned out, he was unduly alarmed about the new German

immigration, for the radicalism of the extremists never pene-
trated the German masses, either here or abroad.

As early as 1847, the *Apologete* reprinted a piece from
the *Philadelphia Demokrat* about the "so-called German
political clubs," in which the writer made the point that some
members were genuine champions of the rights of the German
people but that others were conceited, chronic reformers,
who regarded the German craftsmen as Philistines, and were
"a trial and a burden to the Germans in the United States." [4]
The Methodist Quarterly Review took an equally unfavorable
view of German deists, atheists and pantheists, who "incline
to democracy" but "throw suspicion on Christianity and upon
everything spiritual and religious," circulate the poison of
infidels like David Strauss and Ludwig Feuerbach, and
mistake liberty for license. [5]

In 1852, Professor Gottfried Kinkel, the teacher of Carl
Schurz and one of the dramatic figures of the revolution of
1848, toured the United States to raise funds for another
uprising. The *Apologete* remained cool to his appeal, for it
linked Kinkel with the freethinkers, and contended that communism, socialism and materialism had been responsible for
the failure of the revolution. [6] Two years later, Nast attacked
David Strauss, his former roommate at Tübingen, for sowing
unrest and doubt among the people, while he himself was
"tossed about upon an ocean of philosophical disputation,"
without a haven in which he could find peace and safety. [7] In
a like vein, Nast denounced not only the German freethinking
societies in the United States, but also the Turner clubs,
singing, reading and dramatic organizations which blossomed
into new life in America because of the influence of the Forty-
eighters. He accused them all of spreading the "poison of
so-called progress" and undermining the traditions and cus-

toms of the land which had given them asylum. In language not unlike Bishop Hughes' denunciation of the "Young Irelanders" who settled in the United States after the failure of the Irish uprising of 1848, Nast attacked the radical fringe of the German Forty-eighter immigration. Both Hughes and Nast regarded the newcomers as enemies of religion and the Bible, and Nast was especially enraged by their attacks on the Puritan Sabbath. Indeed, he found merit in a nativist movement which would protect the United States from such contaminating infiltrations from abroad. Nast opposed nativist organizations which operated as secret societies, but he believed that the agitation was primarily directed against Irish Catholics and therefore sympathized with some of the objectives of the native American parties.[8] In contrast with his reaction to Kinkel, Nast was more favorably disposed toward Louis Kossuth, the Hungarian hero of 1848, who also came to America to get dollars for another European Revolution, for he was convinced that Kossuth believed in God and Kinkel did not.[9]

The battle between the *Apologete* and the German freethinkers was long and acrimonious. The radical *Cincinnati Hochwächter* printed a vicious attack on the German Methodists, and Peter Schmucker replied in the *Apologete* with a sharp counterblast.[10] On another occasion, the *Apologete* became involved in a debate with J. A. Försch's *Hahnenruf*, a radical paper published in New York. Karl Heinzen's *Pionier* called the *Apologete* "the organ of the higher idiocy," [11] and to radicals of Heinzen's persuasion, the very word "Methodist" was a term of opprobrium, not only on theological grounds, but because the Methodist Discipline violated all their concepts of personal liberty.

In 1852, Friedrich Hassaurek, who had acquired the

Hochwächter, challenged Nast to a public debate in Mechanics Hall, Cincinnati, on the question whether Christianity was contrary to nature, morality and reason, as many rationalists contended. Hassaurek made the opening address. It was followed by such a tumult from the audience that Nast could not make himself heard, and the argument had to be continued by another Methodist minister and in the respective journals of the two debaters. Nast, the gentle scholar, was no match for his youthful and aggressive opponent, and when he refused to take further part in a public debate, Hassaurek continued the argument for eight nights with another opponent.[12] In 1857, the *Hochwächter* and the *Apologete* indulged in further exchanges about such questions as free will and the nature and power of the devil.[13] The *Turnzeitung*, organ of the German Turner movement, also drew the fire of the *Apologete* for defying time-honored religious customs and beliefs, and the Turner publication replied with an article entitled " Methodist Insanity," which claimed that uneducated ministers were befuddling their listeners with theological hocus pocus.[14] Similar controversies occurred between the Cleveland *Wächter am Erie*, another organ of the rationalists and radicals, and the *Apologete*. In this instance, however, August Thieme, editor of the *Wächter*, granted space for a reply by Nast to an article which the latter regarded as an unfair attack on the Methodist Bible Society.[15]

Enough has been said to reveal Nast's attitude toward some of the leaders of the German immigration of the middle of the last century. He was ready at all times to credit the Forty-eighters with significant cultural, political and intellectual contributions, but he considered their anticlerical rationalism deadly poison and their challenge of American Sabbatarianism an attack on cherished and valuable American traditions. Idealists in politics and social issues the Forty-eighters were, but unfortunately from Nast's viewpoint, they were also exponents of the "higher criticism" and therefore enemies of theology, "materialists on divine revelation," "false prophets of atheism," "Godless men who had no peace." [16]

German-Americans, who had welcomed the revolutionary upheaval of 1848 with high hopes for success, saw the forces of German liberalism crushed under the heels of Prussian grenadiers and the prospects for a German republic indefinitely postponed. The birth of a unified German Empire in 1871, on the other hand, gave them unadulterated joy and satisfaction. Whereas Nast had devoted relatively little space in the *Apologete* to the events of 1848 and 1849, he joined enthusiastically in the almost universal paean of praise that arose from the editorial rooms of America's German-language press when Bismarck, by "blood and iron," accomplished in 1871 what the liberals and intellectuals and common people had failed to bring about in 1848.

In less than a decade, Prussia won three wars, and in 1870, German armies overran France and rolled on into Paris. On the heels of this series of brilliant military triumphs, a new "German spirit" was born not only in the fatherland, but among the German element in the United States. The German-American press and its readers followed with mounting pride the achievements of their blood brothers across the sea. Huge crowds gathered in the leading American cities in 1871 for gigantic victory celebrations, homes in the German sections were decorated with the German colors and torchlight parades and other public demonstrations celebrated the successful culmination of a centuries-old struggle for German unification.

Nast joined wholeheartedly in the adulation of Bismarck,

the builder of empire, and the Hohenzollern king of Prussia who had mounted the throne as emperor of a united Germany. In 1866, Nast had commented unfavorably on the undemocratic character of a Prussia dominated by the *Junker* class and had accused Prussia of provoking war with Austria. But he had been comforted by the thought that Prussia was the home of Protestantism and Austria the bulwark of the medieval, reactionary Papacy; that Bismarck and the seventy-year old king of Prussia could not live forever; and that more progressive ideas would eventually invade the Prussian state.[17] In 1871, he had no reservations. He was sure that Napoleon III and the arrogant French had precipitated the war. The *Apologete* collected funds for the relief of German wounded, followed the military events with remarkable competence, and predicted that the "Lord will bring about a wonderful end" of the war.[18] He believed that the war was worth all it cost the German people, that the huge indemnity imposed upon France was not excessive, and that a long era of peace and good will was about to dawn over Europe.

Like other German-American leaders, Nast also predicted that the war would usher in a new era of greater respect by their American-born neighbors for the German element in the United States. He proudly pointed to the fact that the Germans in America belonged "to the people who conquered Europe's disturber of the peace and who . . . will be the guardians of the peace of Europe and a leader in European civilization." Nast urged his readers to measure up to their new responsibilities as sons and daughters of a great German fatherland and to abandon their mistaken idea that it was their primary function to "initiate Americans into the civilization of Gambrinus and get them to imitate their noisy Sundays."[19]

Nast followed Bismarck's *Kulturkampf* with the Papacy

with great interest and considerable sympathy. He did not like the police and passport regulations of the new Germany, but he maintained that Germany had the right to make her own rules for the preservation of law and order. For weeks after the death of the first German kaiser, the *Apologete* carried accounts of the life of the aged William I, whom Nast described as a noble character and a Christian, and who, along with Bismarck, had but one major objective—to prevent another European war.[20] Nevertheless, Nast understood that the citizens of Germany " will not taste the cup of liberty to the degree that we do in America" but would have to be content with such constitutional privileges as were possible under an hereditary monarchy. He knew that the common man in Germany still had many burdens to bear; and to those who craved greater personal liberty and economic opportunity, he extended a cordial invitation to join the great migration into the American West. Life in America had been completely satisfying for Nast. He was devoted to the American republic, despite the intellectual contacts he maintained with Europe, and he had no hesitation about inviting his fellow Germans to follow his example and make a career for themselves in the United States.

By no means all of Nast's fellow Methodists favored a policy of free and unrestricted immigration to the United States, although it was generally conceded that German immigrants were a valuable addition to the American stock. The *Methodist Review* divided the German immigrants into four classes: the infidels and skeptics; the indifferent and delinquent; the " dupes of Romanism "; and the sober, intelligent and good, who should be welcomed. The cultivated Germans, as far as the *Review* was concerned, were largely of infidel tendency, the illiterates were strongly tinctured with socialism.[21] The Methodist church argued for more and better literature in the German language to be distributed among the new arrivals from Germany and a revitalizing of the missionary effort among immigrants by all evangelical faiths.

The *Apologete* of 1845 described the Methodist mission for immigrants already established in New York and summarized the work carried on at a "ship's mission," a vessel owned by Methodists and tied up to one of the New York piers, where sermons were delivered to newly arrived immigrants, sailors and others, in Swedish, German and English. A German Methodist Emigrant Mission was founded in New York, four years later, with Brother Zwahlen in charge. In 1866, German Methodists planned another harbor mission, and for a time considered buying the Shakespeare Hotel, on the corner of Duane and Williams street, which had been a meeting place for German immigrants and headquarters for the refugees of 1848. Among other functions, the New York mission endeavored to protect new arrivals from dishonest and grasping boardinghouse keepers and from immigrant "runners," who infested the dock areas as employees of railroads and trucking companies and hotel keepers and exploited the immigrant in shameful fashion. Competition among immigrant runners was terrific and many were known as "shoulder hitters," and on several occasions, German missionaries were beaten when they tried to protect immigrants unfamiliar with the language and conditions of American life from these human beasts of prey.

The German Methodist mission sought out the immigrant upon arrival at Castle Garden, provided him with wholesome but cheap food, gave him good advice about lodging, furnished information about opportunities for work, provided letters of introduction to Methodist ministers in the interior if he planned to go west, helped locate friends and relatives, invited him to divine services, and gave him religious literature in the German language, especially Methodist tracts and copies of the New Testament. The New York mission functioned successfully for a number of years but was too far removed from Castle Garden to be completely effective. The property was finally sold, and missionary work was continued in rented quarters near Ellis Island. In 1907, the mission was legally dissolved.

The *Apologete* also published useful data for immigrants, including advertising, immigration statistics, the advantages of becoming naturalized as soon as possible, and instructions on how to acquire American citizenship. It carried invitations from western communities urging German immigrants to settle among them; it explained the terms on which land was available in the Northwest, and the railroad facilities to reach outlying areas. In 1861, several railroad companies, including the Illinois Central and the Hannibal and St. Joseph, ran large advertisements in which they offered homesteads, under attractive conditions, " for the industrious in the garden states of the West." [22] In the issue of April 30, 1857, the *Apologete* described the three possible routes into the interior, and expressed a decided preference for the Baltimore and Ohio, which maintained agents at key points who could speak German, carried immigrants and their baggage on regular trains, instead of in poorly equipped " emigrant trains," provided drinking water and lighted its cars at night.

In the 1850's, the *Apologete* denounced the nativist riots of that turbulent period in American political life and pleaded that religion be kept out of politics. In his denunciation of nativism, Nast included severe criticism of Dennis Kearney, the Irish leader of the anti-Chinese agitation on the west coast in the late 1870's, and denounced Christian churches which condoned the persecution of Chinese immigrants in California. Nast regarded the coolie trade as a new form of slavery, by which employers lured the Chinese to the United States and used them to depress American standards of labor. In 1879, the *Apologete* opposed a Chinese-exclusion bill, as unjust and harmful to both countries, and hoped the President would use his veto power. By 1888, however, it favored immigration restriction and bemoaned the alleged deterioration in the quality of recent arrivals. By this time, Nast had come to share the concern of many Americans about the so-called " new immigration " from eastern and southern Europe and pointed to the high proportion of criminals, saloon keepers, Catholics, anarchists and socialists among them.[23]

Nast was convinced his paper was a useful instrument in the Americanization of German immigrants. His major concern was always with the religious aspects of the problem, but he by no means ignored its other phases. In the summer of 1860, the *Apologete* published a series of articles on United States history, which emphasized that " Christianity is the palladium of this happy Republic." [24] Germans were urged to study the history and institutions of their adopted country so that no cleavage might develop between immigrants and native born. On April 26, 1875, it carried an illuminating article on the hundreth anniversary of the Battle of Lexington and its significance. Other contributions explained how the President was chosen and the intricacies of the electoral college. The first of seventeen articles by Charles Nordhoff, devoted to politics and government, appeared in 1876. Gottlob Nast had translated them into German. They were especially intended for younger readers and were eventually published in book form by Harper's. During the centennial year of

1876, the *Apologete* circulated a German version of the Declaration of Independence, with a plea that Americans return to "the simplicity, honor and faithfulness of the Fathers." [25] In 1879, Nast reprinted an article by Hassaurek, taken from the *Cincinnati Volksblatt*, in which his former religious antagonist described a recent visit to Germany. The article explained why travellers could not feel at home in Germany and why they were so eager to return to the United States. Hassaurek found the fatherland backward and unprogressive, in comparison with America, especially in regard to individual liberties and equality of opportunity. Nast completely approved of the article.

Nast was genuinely proud of the cultural and economic contributions of the German immigrant to America. He urged his fellow countrymen on many occasions to support higher education, art and welfare institutions, so that the United States might become the leader of Western civilization. He was disgusted with immigrants like Friedrich Kapp who grew tired of America, returned to their native land, and published unfavorable reports of life in the country which had given them shelter and opportunity when they were in distress. Nast pleaded with the Germans to keep their intellectual contacts with Europe and preserve their language, their schools and their press in the United States as long as possible, but he realized that ultimately the German element would disappear in the American amalgam. Nast would have liked to have the German language transmitted to the second and third generation, born in America, but he recognized that the Americanization process would make this impossible. Many of his German Methodist confreres in the ministry disagreed with him and accused him of betraying not only his cultural background but the church which he had founded, but Nast was ready to bow to the inevitable and find it good.

As early as 1857, an article in the *Apologete* admitted that children brought up as German Methodists might prefer to listen to preaching in the English language and advised that they be allowed to exercise free choice in the matter.[26] Nast deplored the fact that not enough young men were being recruited for the German ministry, and he regretted the absorption of German Methodist churches by English parishes. He was well aware that with the loss of the language in the second and third generation, the movement he had founded was bound to be absorbed by the English-speaking churches. In 1872, he wrote, " It is the duty of the church to evangelize and not to anglicise," [27] and he urged parents to use German in the home as long as possible. But long before the end of his active career, he conceded that the nation must have a common language, that German private and parochial schools must accept the fact that that language is English, and that parents must cease their criticisms of the American way of life.[28]

By 1924, English was the dominant language in many of the early German churches, and particularly in Sunday schools and young people's societies. By that time, the stream of German immigration had dried up. Older German ministers were requesting transfers from German to English conferences, and no younger ministers were being recruited for the German work. German Methodist churches were rapidly becoming old people's churches. German churches could not compete with the salaries offered by their English brethren. More and more the work of English and German parishes overlapped, and official mergers began in 1924, as the Germans were forced to surrender their separate identity.

The stalwarts of German Methodism fought in vain against Americanization and amalgamation. Nast had foreseen the inevitable. On August 16, 1933, the *Apologete*, in a rare extra edition, announced the end of the Central German Conference, which had been organized nearly seventy years earlier as the first of the German conferences.

10

COLLEGE PRESIDENT

$\mathfrak{B}$oth John Wesley and William Nast enjoyed the benefits of higher education at good European universities. Most of their early co-workers in the vineyard of the Lord could point to no such preparation for ministerial work. The lack of formal education was especially characteristic of many early German Methodist preachers in the United States. The majority came from the humbler walks of life, and many were tradesmen and workmen who had abandoned their jobs to enter the missionary field. Most of them had received a good elementary education in the common schools of Germany, but they knew relatively little about history, the classics, science or philosophy. The sermons, notes and outlines of sermons of some of the pioneers of German Methodism which have been preserved are notable, nevertheless, for their good grammar, clear sentence structure and correct spelling, however deficient they may be in references to the work of scholars.

In the early days of American Methodism, when preachers were asked where they had prepared for the ministry, they often replied, without apology or embarrassment, " In Brush College." The libraries of many itinerants were limited to such tracts and religious books as they could stuff into their saddlebags. Peter Cartwright, veteran Methodist circuit rider, boasted that of the thousands of local preachers and circuit riders, not fifty had more than a common school education; many had less, and not one had been trained in a theological school. Salaries were pitifully low and there was little money available for books, and as a consequence, the narrow theology of some of the early preachers became even narrower.

In 1846, the *Apologete* provided a list of books which Methodist preachers were urged to read and study in preparation for their evangelical mission. For the first year, Wesley's catechism, Jacoby's treatise on Christian faith, a tract on church polity, and a German grammar were recommended. This course of reading was to be followed in the second year with Fletcher's *Appeal*, Bogue on the Holy Scriptures and Collier's *Introduction to Holy Scripture*, and more on church polity and German grammar and composition. It was recommended that each minister write out at least one sermon in full so that he could apply the lessons in composition which he had learned.

It took a long time to break down the notion that higher education somehow was not very helpful and even incompatible with the main job of winning souls for German Methodism. As late as the 1870's, there were still preachers with strong prejudices against colleges and theological seminaries. "Happy that our church," wrote one minister, "has not yet prescribed for the Lord where he should get his servants, whether from the plow, the worker's bench, or an institution of learning."[1] Another critic of higher education wrote disparagingly of the craving for honorary degrees, and insisted that it was better to write S. S. ("Sinner Saved") after one's name than LL. D. or D. D.[2] Engelhardt Riemenschneider, one of the early German Methodist leaders, commented in 1881, "Before I could finish five years of study, I might have saved hundreds of precious souls."[3] Even those who admitted the desirability of a better education always insisted that its true value depended upon the stress it put upon faith and God's mercy. "Experience shows," wrote one contributor to the *Apologete* near the close of Nast's editorship, "that most ministers who come from the universities have lost touch with the people because of their training, methods of thinking and views of life." He went on to argue that the work of the German Methodist church had to be done primarily among the common people, and the only preparation necessary was knowledge of Holy Writ and a genuine passion to save souls.[4]

Nast would have agreed that the primary function of his church was to save souls from sin and damnation, but as a scholar, with wide intellectual interests, he could not agree with the brethren who saw no need for Methodist colleges and seminaries. He began to advocate a German professorship in affiliation with an existing college, and then, the founding of a German Methodist college, with a complete curriculum. To these two ends, the *Apologete* tried consistently to direct the attention of its readers.

In 1859, when the first conference of German Methodist preachers assembled in Chicago, Nast was chosen to preside over its deliberations. Among the many items of business was a discussion of the need for more schools and colleges, and a committee of five, with Nast as a member, was selected to formulate plans to meet the educational requirements of the church. The conference approved a proposal to publish a book, to sell for not more than a dollar, to help ministers prepare better sermons, and Nast was active on this project also. The group favored day schools to train teachers, endorsed a plan to found a German professorship at Baldwin University in Berea, Ohio, and promised to support Quincy College in Illinois, a pioneer Methodist institution. Finally, a beginning was made on the collection of material for a history of German Methodism, and circuit riders were requested to record their experiences.[5] Four years later, the Missionary Society of the Methodist Church admitted the need for better educated teachers and preachers, and gave its attention to plans to support the German professorship in Berea, and for a theological seminary, to be established somewhat further west.[6]

In 1853, the trustees of Asbury University in Greencastle, Indiana, authorized a new chair of German language and literature and offered the appointment to Nast. The incumbent was also expected to teach Hebrew, a language in which Nast was fully qualified. Nast agreed to accept the appointment, provided the Methodist book committee would release him from his duties as editor of the *Apologete*. On August 12, 1853, Nast announced his resignation from the paper, and prepared to move his family to Indiana. One of the attractions of the new position was his belief that as a professor he could devote more time to his *magnum opus*, a scholarly commentary on the New Testament, than he could while charged with the heavy duties of editor of the *Apologete*.

The call to Greencastle depended upon selling enough scholarship rights at one hundred dollars a certificate to finance the new chair, and since only seven were sold, Nast remained at his editor's desk.[7]

Nast's interest now turned, with renewed energy, to the question of a German professorship in Berea, Ohio, to be connected with Baldwin University, which had been opened in 1845 and incorporated as a university in 1856. Three years earlier, in 1853, the German Methodists had established in Quincy, Illinois, what was really a high school which bore the proud name of a German-English Seminary. Jakob Rothweiler may deserve the credit for having first suggested a German department at Berea, but Nast gave the project his enthusiastic and consistent support, and the publicity he gave it in the *Apologete* contributed greatly to its success.

The trustees of Baldwin University agreed to add a German department as soon as the German Methodists could raise $10,000, and so Rothweiler took to the road and called on German congregations in many parts of the Middle West, selling scholarship rights in perpetuity for a hundred dollars. In May 1857, the *Apologete* reported that German ministers had subscribed for forty of these scholarships, and when sixty more had been sold, the professorship could be established. The appointment to the professorship was originally offered to John C. Lyon of New York, a forceful preacher and an able linguist, but he refused to come when he learned that he would be expected to spend his summer vacations raising money for his salary and other expenses.[8] The post thereupon went to Professor O. Henning, who resigned after the first year to go to Allegheny College, with his salary still $53.25 in arrears. In 1859, Rothweiler became both German professor and financial agent for Baldwin University. He was expected to augment his salary by preaching in neighboring communities. Meantime, "Brother Baldwin" had agreed to erect a three-story building to be known as "German Hall." On the first floor the professor and his family had their living quarters; the second story was devoted to classrooms and a chapel, and the third served as a dormitory for students.[9]

When the German department was officially opened on August 12, 1858, the *Apologete* urged German parents to send their children to Berea, because the college offered them instruction in both German and English in a thoroughly Christian environment. Twelve German students attended the first classes, and an equal number of English-speaking students took advantage of the opportunity to attend German classes, for all students were entitled to all the privileges of Baldwin University. Board cost $1.75 to $2.25 a week, and rooms were available in private homes in the town for as little as twenty-five cents a week. In June 1859, Nast delivered the baccalaureate sermon at Berea, in English, and in the afternoon, preached in German to an audience of sixty. At the close of the year, the Northern Ohio Conference elected him a member of the board of trustees of Baldwin University.

Berea, a few miles from the rapidly growing Cleveland, and now virtually a part of its metropolitan area, originally had been planned as a backwoods Utopia. The land on which it stood once belonged to Gideon Granger, Jefferson's postmaster general. John Baldwin, one of the three founders of the community, was the son of a veteran of the American Revolution. He had taught school in the East, become an exhorter and had caught the "Ohio fever." In 1827, he bought two hundred acres in northeastern Ohio, where he became a successful frontier farmer, and a manufacturer of "Berea grindstones," an industry which later gave the town its name as the grindstone city of the world. Baldwin was a rugged, thrifty, independent Yankee, an able businessman and a devoutly religious man, who attracted attention at his house-raising in Berea when he violated one of the strongest frontier traditions by refusing to serve liquor to those who came to help with the work.

As early as 1835, Baldwin had considered establishing an institution of higher education and a model town community. In 1836, he encountered two Methodist ministers, who became co-founders of his Berea community. They were Henry O. Sheldon and James Gilruth, prohibitionists, pacifists and abolitionists, interested in establishing a town on Biblical lines which would become the center for the conversion of the rest of the world. The three men drew up an agreement by which all property would be held in common, and all business carried on for the benefit of a common treasury. Berea was to be a strictly "Christian community," dedicated to perfectionism and millenialism. This "Community of United Christians," consisting at the outset of only three families, was officially established in 1836. The name Berea was chosen by an "inward voice," heard by Sheldon. A charter for a seminary was obtained from the Ohio legislature. Within a year, over thirty additional families joined the community, and a long constitution, consisting of a Scriptural preamble and twenty-five articles, was adopted. It prescribed total abstention from liquor, coffee, tea and tobacco. Government was entrusted to an elected board of twelve. A crop failure, internal dissension, and the devastating effects of the panic of 1837 soon brought an end to this experiment in communitarian living, and thereafter each member decided to farm and work for himself. The Methodist Seminary was started in Berea in 1844, however, and in 1853, Baldwin

University was established. This was the little Ohio community with which the German Methodists made their closest connection, and to which Nast eventually moved his family.[10]

Five years after the establishment of a German department at Baldwin University, the trustees of that institution offered the German Methodists a separate building, the gift of James Wallace, for a German college, provided they would organize a board of trustees and raise $10,000 for another professorship. On June 3, 1863, a number of German preachers and laymen met in Berea to consider the offer. They began their deliberations with song and prayer and an address by Professor A. Liebenstein. Thereupon articles were prepared for the incorporation of "German Wallace College" of Berea, and thirteen trustees, with revolving terms of one, two and three years, were chosen and authorized to solicit gifts and to sell tuition scholarships. It was suggested that members of the several German Methodist bodies be requested to make a per capita contribution of one dollar and a half, and the delegates in attendance made a beginning by contributing twenty-eight dollars.

Nast was a member of the original board of trustees of Wallace College, and was elected to serve both as president of the board and president of the faculty. Jakob Rothweiler, to whom Nast referred several times as "the real founder," was chosen vice-president, and since he was in residence in Berea, the major burden of administration fell upon him. In 1864, Wallace College, the first German Methodist college in the United States, opened its doors, with the patriarch of German Methodism as its first president. The enrollment in the first year was forty. The first woman graduate was Nast's daughter, Fanny. It is estimated that as Fanny Nast Gamble her benefactions to various church activities eventually totalled three million dollars, and she bestowed many gifts upon the college in Berea, including an auditorium which bears her name, and endowment funds for a Nast chair of theology and a theological department known as the Nast Theological Seminary.

The two sister institutions of Baldwin and Wallace continued under separate boards of trustees until their merger in 1913, but from the first there was complete reciprocity between them so that students could take courses in either. In 1870, when the assets of Wallace College exceeded $77,000, James Wallace gave the institution a hundred and fifty acres of quarry land on Drummond Island, valued at $1,000. The first faculty, in 1864, consisted of Rothweiler, who was professor of the German language and Biblical literature; B. W. Mosblech, who taught ancient and modern languages; Nast's son Albert, who was teacher of piano, and Mary Hasenpflug who taught the melodeon. Teachers' salaries ranged from $500 to $700 for the year, and each instructor taught from six to eight hours a day. A campaign was launched immediately to raise $25,000 among the German churches for a chair of theology, and a number of English-speaking congregations made generous contributions.

Wallace College opened its doors while the country was still involved in the Civil War. The institution had to face several acute financial crises in its early years. Nevertheless, enrollment grew steadily, although the institution always remained comparatively small. A few members of the first student groups turned out to be poor material for college and several were disciplinary cases, but this experience was typical of many colleges, including the church supported. To the great satisfaction of the founders, a considerable number of the graduates of Wallace College entered the ministry. In

1872, the college was recognized by the General Methodist Conference as an " official seminary " of the church, and by 1905, three hundred of the alumni were preachers and thirty had become college teachers.

For several decades the college struggled with the problems of finance, and Nast published many pleas in the *Apologete* for more generous support from the German Methodists. He sought money for new buildings, for a respectable library and for the improvement of faculty salaries. Rothweiler spent much of 1865 touring the Middle West to raise money and get pledges of support, and it became the general practice for the vice-president to serve as chief money-raiser for the institution. In 1875, the new vice-president, Rev. P. F. Schneider, visited dozens of German churches, to sell certificates of scholarship, signed by President Nast. In return for a donation of a hundred dollars, the donor had the right to send one of his offspring to the college on a free tuition basis. Apparently, the agreement was made in perpetuity, a common practice of many colleges at the time. Schneider and his predecessors and successors, who preached in many churches on behalf of the little college, always followed their sermons with appeals for a special collection to support the struggling institution. One can get some notion of the relative poverty of German Methodist congregations in the decade after the Civil War, when one finds that collections of $15 in Dayton, Ohio, and of $30 in Covington, Kentucky, were considered especially good. Some contributions were as small as fifty cents, but large or small, the names of the donors were gratefully recorded in the *Apologete*. In 1879, the college sold group pictures of Nast and the Wallace College faculty to help clear a debt of $7,000, and every one who donated $10 or more, received a large photograph free.

In 1868, the Northwest Conference sent Friedrich Kopp of Milwaukee to inspect the college. He found an institution consisting of two major buildings. One, a brick structure, had a large lecture room, which also served as a chapel, on the first floor, and on the second floor, a meager library and a little exhibit of natural history, the gift of the geologist Hermann Herzer, to whom Wallace College gave its first honorary degree, a Master of Arts, in 1869. The second building, Baldwin Hall, was a dormitory for students, and provided living quarters for one professor and a family who did the cooking. A third building, which housed a number of orphan children, was soon to be converted into a dormitory for women students. The college also owned several smaller houses in the village, which were rented to private families. The campus occupied about six acres in the heart of Berea.

Kopp reported that a student could feed himself at Berea for a little under $2 a week. In 1873, total expenses for a year's residence were estimated between $125 and $150. Kopp found that Rev. Friedrich Schuler, the vice-president, was actually in charge of administration because Nast spent most of his time on his editorial duties in Cincinnati. The faculty included Professor Liebenstein, described as "a solid, German scholar" and Philip Welker, professor of modern languages and music, soon to be joined by Karl Riemenschneider, who was completing his work for the doctor's degree at Tübingen. Kopp attended the examinations, which were held in German at the end of the term. The students were examined in logic, German, English, Latin, composition, religion, singing and penmanship, and Kopp was favorably impressed by the original work of a number of students in the field of rhetoric. Some students were studying algebra, geometry and astronomy under the reciprocal agreement with Baldwin University. Because

Wallace College needed a good piano for the work in music, President Nast sought contributions from friends in the East, and persuaded Steinway to give the college a discount of $150 on a new instrument. Student life seemed wholesome and normal, and the Schiller and Germania clubs were flourishing among the student body. One critical item in the inspector's report referred to the "too flimsy covering of arms and breasts" by some of the women students at Baldwin, as "not quite fitting for moral, virtuous daughters of Methodists." [11]

For a number of years, the *Apologete* published the full curriculum of Wallace College, including the offerings of a preparatory department, and courses in sciences, such as chemistry and geology, mathematics through calculus, and classics and theology. For an extra fee, students could take instruction in music, drawing and business subjects. All students were required to take courses in religion and penmanship, and many subjects, including arithmetic and geography, originally were taught in the German language. The curriculum provided for a four-year college course, and a two-year course in the seminary. Work in the preparatory department was designed to cover one year. The catalogue of 1872, issued jointly by Baldwin and Wallace, showed that the former had twelve faculty members and 326 students, and the latter a faculty of five and a student body of 102. After the German fashion, examinations were conducted for some years at Wallace in public. Accounts of activities at the college almost invariably contained references to revivals and conversions which were in progress among the student body.

The hard times following the panic of 1873 left many colleges in grave financial difficulties, and Wallace College was no exception. By 1877, the enrollment had dropped to seventy-five, and a number of students went home before the end of the term because their funds were exhausted or to find a job, although by modern standards, their costs were surprisingly low. In 1874, the *Apologete* published an estimate of costs for one term at Wallace College, which budgeted $23 to $25 for food, and $3.24 for a room in a student dormitory. One to three dollars were charged for tuition, and a two-dollar fee for the janitor; firewood cost sixty-seven cents, and thirty cents were charged for light. One to three dollars was the estimated cost for books, paper and incidentals, bringing the total to either $31.21 or $37.21 for the term.[12]

Compared with the manifold duties of modern college presidents it cannot be said that Nast was very active as president of Wallace College. He was devoted to the institution, but he was unable to spend much time in residence in Berea, for his major responsibility was the *Apologete* in Cincinnati, and he had to support Wallace College largely at long range. He gave the college much publicity; his paper repeatedly pleaded for additional funds to develop the school, and in every financial campaign Nast gave generously of his own meager funds. Several times he expressed a desire to teach at the college, whenever his term as editor might expire, but his wish was never realized.

Nast presided at meetings of the board—to buy land for the college, to devise a curriculum, and to design an appropriate seal for the new institution. He was on the committee which drafted the by-laws for the college, and on the standing committee on ways and means. He usually attended the annual board meeting in June, presented the diplomas at the commencement exercises, and on a number of occasions, delivered the baccalaureate sermon. But the real direction of the everyday affairs of the college was in the hands of a succession of vice-presidents who also were the financial agents for the institution. In 1881, Nast agreed to give Bible lectures on Sunday afternoons to the students, and in 1888, he announced that he had bequeathed his library to the college. In 1888, he concurred with his fellow trustees in rejecting an invitation from the board of trustees of Baldwin to unite the two institutions, believing that such a merger was not yet necessary or desirable. As a very old man, Nast was still attending commencements in the early 1890's, although he could no longer deliver long addresses. He generally pronounced the benediction, and was referred to still as " the nominal president" of Wallace College.[13] By this time, Vice-president Karl Riemenschneider was in actual charge, and the *Apologete* referred to him as " the functioning president." Perhaps Nast's greatest service to the college was to lend it the prestige of his name. No one was more revered in German Methodist circles, and the fact that Wallace College had Nast's support was of inestimable benefit during the institution's early critical years.

The German Methodists founded and supported schools and charitable institutions in other states also, and although Nast's primary interest was in Berea, the *Apologete* reported regularly on their progress. Considering their relatively small numbers and their modest financial resources, the record of the German Methodists in supporting educational and eleemosynary institutions was truly remarkable, when compared with the achievements of their more prosperous English-speaking brethren in American Methodism.

The German school at Quincy, Illinois, stemmed largely from the labors of Hermann Koch, a Prussian who had studied medicine in Germany, farmed in Missouri and then had turned to teaching. The Quincy school was a coeducational bilingual institution. In 1864, it was moved to Warrenton, Missouri, and renamed Central Wesleyan College. A theological school was added, and Koch served the institution until 1895.[14] A German Methodist normal school was started in Galena, Illinois, in 1868, moved to Charles City, Iowa, in 1891, and finally amalgamated with Morningside College in Sioux City. A German department at Mt. Pleasant, Iowa, was for a time affiliated with Iowa Wesleyan and finally united with Central Wesleyan in Warrenton, Missouri. Several attempts to establish schools in Texas failed, but in 1881, Blinn Memorial College was opened in Brenham, Texas. St. Paul's College in St. Paul, Minnesota, was another institution supported by German Methodists, and there were still other smaller schools which had to be discontinued after a few years. The high point in the number of German Methodist educational institutions was reached in 1910, with about one hundred teachers, over fifteen hundred students, and combined assets of over $1,000,000. The financial status of some institutions was always precarious, and the standards sometimes did not exceed those of a secondary school, but the consistent support they received from German Methodists through the years testifies to the real devotion to religion and education by a group whose worldly goods were never plentiful.[15]

The German Methodist church also supported old people's homes, such as the *Altenheim* of Quincy, Illinois, opened in 1890 as a project of the St. Louis German Conference, the Bethany *Altenheim* in Brooklyn, opened in 1909 to serve the East German Conference, the Bethesda *Altenheim* of Cincinnati, and the *Altenheim* of Los Angeles. Many of these institutions were finally integrated with the English conferences.[16]

The German Methodists founded a Central Wesleyan

Orphan Asylum in Warrenton, Missouri, in 1864. In the same year, the German Methodist Orphans Home of Berea, Ohio, was established. Nast had urged such an institution in the *Apologete* as early as 1850, and he followed its progress with great interest. On May 2, 1864, the Berea orphanage opened its doors to eight children. In 1917, it cared for one hundred and fifteen, and had developed the " cottage system " instead of housing the children in one large building. Religious instruction was a major concern of the institution, which combined emphasis upon the Methodist gospel with a program of vocational training. In its early years, the guiding spirit of the Berea orphanage was Rev. W. Ahrens, who moved to the community in 1863, and with the help of Rothweiler managed to acquire a house and four acres of land for $1,400. Although he had a family of six to support, Ahrens' annual salary was $300. In 1869, the orphans were moved into a new building, with a capacity for fifty children. Nast was a member of the advisory committee of the orphanage, and his wife served on the visiting committee. In 1903, when a new building was dedicated, providing two hundred beds, Albert Nast, son of one of the institution's earliest supporters, made the dedicatory address.[17]

The deaconess movement, with " mother houses " in several American cities, was an importation from Switzerland and Germany, which German Methodists imitated and developed in the United States. Its greatest progress occurred after Nast's death, although the *Apologete* had given it its support while Nast was still editor. Among other objectives, it trained young women for social-service work, nursing and teaching in kindergarten. The Elizabeth Gamble Deaconess House was opened in Cincinnati in 1888, and although sponsored by English-speaking Methodists, it admitted young women from the German churches to its training course. Louise Golder was the first German Methodist deaconess trained in the United States, and in 1896, the German General Conference sponsored a " mother house " in Cincinnati, with Miss Golder as its head.[18]

11

THEOLOGIAN AND AUTHOR

𝕴n 1882, in a letter to his father, Albert Nast observed that "all Methodism is in a process of fermentation from which I trust eventually we will get the pure wine of reason and moderation." The father was always deeply concerned with the tenets and practices of his faith, and as a scholar, he thought he could help establish his church on ever firmer foundations by his own research and writing. Nast's publications attracted attention not only in German circles, but in the Methodist church as a whole.

To Nast, John Wesley's career and writings were of course fundamental, as they were to Methodists everywhere. Nast gladly accepted the belief that Wesley had developed his movement from the principles of the Lutheran Reformation. Wesley remained one of his favorite authors. Another was John W. Fletcher (de la Fléchère), son of a Genevan army officer who had been converted to Wesleyanism in England and whom Wesley, his friend for forty years, called the best defender of Methodist principles. Nast referred frequently to Fletcher's works. Among leading German theologians, Nast preferred Dr. Friedrich August Tholuck, a professor at the University of Halle and a bitter foe of rationalism, and from his works Nast made numerous abstracts, translations and quotations.

Nast's views on the basic principles of Methodist Christianity could be assembled easily from his voluminous contributions to the *Apologete* over a period of fifty years. Many of his articles eventually found their way into the fourteen books which Nast published during his lifetime. In addition, he delivered hundreds of sermons during his long career as a minister. The refinements of some of his theological discussions can be understood only by fellow specialists in the field, but the basic principles of his faith are rather easily summarized, for despite his wide learning, Nast was a simple, pious soul, with a faith that could not be shaken by "the higher criticism."

For Nast, the Bible was the inspired word of God, not to be questioned and to be accepted in all its parts. Although many passages might require exposition by theologians, he never questioned the basic fact that the book was the perfect revelation of God to man. Nast had no sympathy with the rationalists who flourished in German universities, and he believed the rationalist movement was infecting the evangelical churches of America, as it had corrupted Lutheranism on the Continent. Nast opposed the " unjustifiable principle of interpretation which constitutes the essence of rationalism " and was especially incensed by its denial of Biblical prophecies as yet unfulfilled. In the *Methodist Review* of 1890, he de-

nounced the " arrogance of rationalism to decide which state-
ments may be taken in their simple grammatical sense and
which must be made to mean what they do not say." [1] For
Nast it was all or none. The Bible needed only to be read
in simple literalness in order for its divine origin to be appreciated.

At the center of God's plan for the redemption of man
from original sin stood the loving, compassionate figure of
Jesus, the Saviour. He sat at God's right hand, guiding and
directing everything that affected man's career on earth. Men
could find peace and salvation only " in the blood of the
lamb." " A living faith in Jesus Christ and his Holy Word,"
Nast wrote in the preface to his *Commentary* on the New
Testament,[2] " is not the work of a logical demonstration to
the understanding but that of an attestation of the Holy Ghost
to the conscience and heart." Faith required that men believe
that Christ was God manifest in the flesh; " the philosophy
of the fact we must leave to God." [3]

In *The Methodist Quarterly Review* for 1860, Nast reviewed the work of a number of German theologians, cited
Scripture, and indulged in several excursions into metaphysics,
to prove that Jesus was both God and man, and that his dual
personality was not a mystery, self-contradictory, or transcend-
ing human reason. He expounded " the personal union of the
Logos and of the human nature in Christ" and stressed
Christ's twofold nature. But after he finished with logic and
metaphysics, Nast returned to the position that man could
not fathom the mystery of Christ's being, but must, as a sacred
duty, " learn to understand so much of it as the Scriptures
enable us to know and as we can comprehend without affect-
ing our faith in the fact on which the mystery is based." [4]

Nast rejected many details of both the Lutheran and the

Reformed positions. He contended that the Son of God could become man without thereby destroying his true divinity, that Christ remained conscious of his dual nature even while functioning as a man upon earth, and that "only so much of his divine self-consciousness *as was necessary for his mediatorial office* passed over into his human self-consciousness." Nast preferred "the unfathomable depth of this mystery to any philosophical solution of the problem." To him, Jesus was the Son of God and the Saviour of mankind. With the same unquestioning faith, he accepted the bodily resurrection of all men, for he believed it was based upon the Word of God and buttressed by the fact of Jesus' rise from the dead. He admitted that finite minds could not explain the mystery, but again he accepted the fact, without question, and contended that the resurrected body will grow from man's earthly body and retain its individual identity through eternity.[5]

In the Methodist faith, conversion was the great central experience in a person's religious life, the key to salvation, and the promise of a life everlasting. This religious phenomenon, however mysterious it may seem to those who have not experienced it, was very real to those who had. To try to describe it for others in theological or psychological terms remains more or less a fruitless undertaking. According to Nast, however, conversion was but the first step to complete sanctification. It was only the initial rebirth, and a choice of the free will, but the heart had as yet not won a complete victory over all the sinful elements in man's character which held him in the clutches of worldliness. In endless exchanges with contributors to the *Apologete,* Nast belabored his concept of sanctification and tried to explain it to his fellow religionists. According to him, the converted had not yet attained the "full life in Christ." Sanctification, which would have to follow, apparently was not "something different in nature from regeneration" but only different in degree. It was the process of becoming perfect as God is perfect and in accordance with His will.

Farther than this it was impossible for Nast to go, and many readers must have had difficulty following his involved arguments on this question. He was convinced that a life of fundamental piety would dispel all doubt and obviate the necessity for closer definition. The answers to all questions were in the Bible, and it called for repentance before salvation, made it clear that no man could save himself and that to try to do so was only risking damnation. To him, sanctification was a fact and not a theory; it could be experienced and demonstrated; and it was more a matter of the heart than of the head.[6]

According to Nast, salvation depended entirely upon the mercy and saving grace of a Heavenly Father. Like the Lutherans, he believed in justification by faith and in the covenant of grace which God is ever ready to make with mortal men and by which man may receive forgiveness from sin, "in and for the merits of the Lord Jesus." Christ's atonement is the central theme in the religious drama, and divine grace is available to all who seek it. God was a very personal being and Nast felt extraordinarily close to both the Father and the Son. From this close relationship, he received the "full assurance of acceptance," was convinced that he was doing the Lord's work, and like many others believed he could "enjoy full salvation."

Prayer was a vital part of every Methodist experience meeting, and stress upon its efficacy was as central to Nast's beliefs as the necessity for conversion or salvation. As late as 1892, he wrote a series of articles on " The Fact of Prayer " for the *Apologete*, which represented an abridgment from a scholarly work on prayer by a German theologian, in which Nast attempted to simplify the latter's views for the ordinary reader.[7] Ludwig Nippert wrote similar digests of larger works on the meaning and practice of prayer for readers of the *Apologete*, and Nast, throughout his long editorship, gave the subject as much space as any other religious topic in his paper.

Nast believed that everything that happened, in the universe or in the life of an individual, was according to the Lord's will, and therefore pre-arranged. This conclusion brought the founder of German Methodism very close to the Presbyterian doctrine of predestination. In 1875, he wrote his son Albert, " It will appear very strange to you that of late Calvinism appears to me in an entirely different aspect from what it has been represented by Methodist writers. I cannot help thinking we have done great injustice to it." [8] Birth, death, good and bad fortune, and all the accidents of life had to be accepted as God's will, and as part of His plans. Nast applied this belief literally and in simple trust to all that befell him in life. In 1858, for example, when he was injured in a fall from the depot platform at Lawrenceburg, Indiana, while getting out of a train in the dark, he reported the accident in the *Apologete* as an act of the Lord and concluded with a prayer that he might be able to accept whatever came from the throne of grace.[9]

The *Apologete* also engaged in many theological disputations about death, the Last Judgment and immortality. " Put your house in order, for you will surely die," was Nast's constant admonition to his readers. He discussed such theoretical questions as what happens after death, where the soul goes, and its status as it waits for the Second Coming and the Last Judgment.[10] Apparently he believed that immediately after death the souls of the saved were released from sin and struggle, took up residence with Christ, saw "the King in his beauty," and enjoyed all the wonderful things God had prepared for them.[11] He never tired of writing learned expositions of Bible passages dealing with such matters, and one wonders how many readers were able to follow his labored discussions. The basic concept, however, which underlay all his theology was that only the complete acceptance of Christ could insure man's release from the penalty of eternal death. Only babies were exempted from this stern law of salvation, for he could not approve of a doctrine which condemned little children to damnation simply because they had not as yet arrived at an age when they could seek salvation for themselves. He also wrote extensively about baptism and its relation to the process of salvation. When children died young, he believed it was according to God's plan, and he comforted readers with the assurance that "innocent children, plucked like lilies," are immediately transported to heaven and their death must therefore be accepted as a "sweet" experience.

Immortality was a subject on which he admitted no debate. Heaven, in his theology, was a specific place, inhabited by the souls of specific individuals whose identity would endure throughout eternity. When his little grandson was seriously ill from candy which he had received "from a visiting Irish lady," the patience with which the boy bore his illness so impressed Nast that he wrote the boy's parents, "It made me feel even a little uneasy, whether the Lord might not intend to prepare the little lamb for the heavenly pastures." [12] Ludwig Nippert, writing from Europe in 1856, reporting the illnesses in his family, commented almost joyously, "We already have a little son in heaven." [13] When ministers died, the obituaries referred to the "rejoicing there will be up there, when these old heroes of German Methodism meet again in Paradise."

What I have said thus far in explanation of Nast's theological position is derived primarily from the *Apologete*. Discussion of some of these subjects ran serially for several months, some were incorporated in the books which Nast published, some were mere translations or abridgments from other authors. Despite his heavy editorial duties and the many demands upon his time as a preacher, he could not resist the scholar's instinct to write books, which would present his ideas in more permanent fashion. Several of his books deserve some analysis here.

In German Methodist circles, Nast was often referred to as "the creator of our German literature," and if we include the books he edited, he had no less than fourteen to his credit. Not all were significant, and few represented original contributions. They were primarily compilations and digests of other authors, but they reveal his wide acquaintance with the literature of theology and religion on two continents and a familiarity with the work of scholars who wrote in several foreign languages, which Nast read in the original.

Nast's biography of John Wesley may be considered first, although it was less significant than several of Nast's other books. It was neither a history of Methodism nor a biography of its founder, but rather a brief account of the development of the Methodist movement, with some references to its methods and the difficulties it encountered in its early years. It was based almost wholly on the work of three authors, who had written in English, the substance of whose books Nast translated and condensed for his own little volume. He made no claim to originality; only the arrangement of the material and a few additional comments were his own. A collection of Wesley's sermons, which Nast translated into German and published in 1850, had been the forerunner of the Wesley biography of some three hundred pages, which appeared in Cincinnati in 1852 and was advertised in the *Apologete* at seventy cents a copy, with a discount to preachers.[14]

A similar work of revision for an American printing, without any original contributions from the editor, was Nast's edition of Christian Heinrich Zeller's *Kurze Seelenlehre, gegründet auf Schrift und Erfahrung, für Eltern, Prediger und Lehrer* (Brief Instructions for the Soul, Based on Scripture and Experience, for Parents, Ministers and Teachers), which was published as a 235-page book in Cincinnati. This treatise, planned as a pedagogical handbook with instructions for the soul, opens with discussions of the physical and spiritual nature of man and proceeds, with many references to Biblical passages, from the creation of man and the fall, by which one person brought sin into the world, to the method for man's final redemption. The book reveals a fundamentalist approach and is based on the most literal acceptance of every word in the Bible.

Equally interesting, however, are the author's excursions into physiology and psychology. Zeller deals with man's anatomical and physiological nature in detail, including the nervous system, the digestive tract, and the sex organs, which he thought were intimately connected with the digestive system. Sin he considered the cause of all the body's ailments, which came into the world with Adam's fall. There is a long discussion of the five senses and their relation to the soul, whose activities are described in terms which to-day would apply more specifically to the workings of the mind. Some of the author's physiology and psychology is sound; much of it sounds fantastic to modern scientists. The book also deals somewhat with psychic problems and mental health, especially those of the "un-converted" and the "un-reborn." There are sections on heredity, the influence of climate on the soul, the condition of the soul before and after death, and the atonement process. Zeller maintains that the departed can return to earth, but he denounces spiritualism because he thinks it sinful to ask advice from the dead. The book closes with a discussion of the only true religion, as revealed by God in the person of Jesus, whose sacrifice provided the means of salvation. The style is in good German, and the book is a curious mixture of theology, science and pseudo-science. Nast believed it was an important book, which merited the time and labor necessary to prepare an American edition. He was particularly fascinated by its medical and psychological sections, for he always was interested in such matters and in his early years had hoped to prepare for the practice of medicine.

Nast's *Philosophie des Erlösungsplans* (Philosophy of the Plan of Salvation) (Cincinnati, 1858) was announced as a book by an American citizen, revised for German readers from an English edition, by W. Nast, D. D. The original had appeared sixteen years earlier, but there is no indication of who the author was. Dr. Calvin E. Stowe wrote an introduction to Nast's edition, the main purpose of which was to prove that only the Christian religion could meet man's spiritual needs.

Beginning with learned references to the pantheism and idolatry of ancient times, the argument undertakes to show that no human power could free man from evil, and that a revelation of holiness was needed, through divine intervention. Nast follows the story of the evolution of God's plan for men from the miracles of Moses and the monotheism of the Israelites to the perfect revelation in the person of Jesus. He knew his Hebrew and ancient history, and the book reveals considerable mastery of etymology and linguistics, as he shows how language evolved from an expression of mere material things to a means of conveying abstract ideas.

Nast regarded selfishness, a craving for worldly power, and jealousy as man's worst sins. Jesus had rejected them all for humility and compassion. Nast argued that to obey God without loving Him would be degrading, and that conduct was not the test of salvation. Man left to himself was totally inadequate; he had to realize his lost state and seek support from on high. To reject God's mercy meant loss of body and soul and consignment to "eternal fire," without even a drop of water to alleviate the pain. Every one was "a guilty and damned creature" and could be saved only by the love of Jesus. From his condemnation of the ancient philosophers who extolled human wisdom and conduct, Nast excepted only Socrates and Plato, but he admitted that Confucius, Seneca and others taught moral mandates strikingly like those of the New Testament.

In this book, prayer is described as the "assimilation" of the man who prays with Him to whom he prays. Prayer is to be practiced as a sacred duty and a means of grace; prayers must be long and fervent, and reveal complete faith and dependence on God. Among other media to stir the Christian virtues, Nast gives high rank to music and poetry. He gives advice about preaching to his fellow ministers and insists that every listener be made aware of his guilt and danger, before proceeding with an explanation of the process of salvation. By faith alone man's spirit can be brought into communion with God. "Without revealed truth, reason has no basis, belief is untrue and conscience spoiled." The book ends with a plea to desert the "sinful and destructive philosophy" of pantheists and deists and follow Christ. Nast quotes liberally from the great thinkers of all ages, from Plato and the Stoics to Erasmus, and cites history, astronomy and science to develop his thesis, but his final authority remains the Bible. One wonders how many readers were able to master the book's many difficult passages, the style, moreover, being involved and complicated. An anonymous reviewer from Worcester, Massachusetts, writing in *The Methodist Quarterly Review*, took issue with some of the author's conclusions and apparently regarded his many references to the scholars and philosophers of earlier times as proof that Nast at one time in his life must have been a skeptic.

In 1867, Poe and Hitchcock of Cincinnati published Nast's revision of the *Christologische Betrachtungen nach Dr. van Oosterzee's Bild Christi* (Christological Observations based on Dr. van Oosterzee's Picture of Christ).[15] Harper's and Scribner's, much to Nast's chagrin, had refused to publish an English translation. In this volume of 275 pages, we have another example of how Nast reworked the findings of European theological scholarship. It deals with the old familiar themes—how the Godhead and man were united in the person of Jesus, as Lord and Saviour. Nast repeats his familiar thesis, that here is a mystery which man can never completely grasp but which is nevertheless true because Scripture says it is and because the heart of the man of faith feels it, though he lacks the scientific terminology to explain it. Nast revised the form of Oosterzee's treatise, abridged parts of it, and made additions from American sources. Part of the book is in the style of a catechism, with formal questions and long answers. The book reviews all the forecasts of the coming of the Messiah, from ancient mythology and Mexican legends through the Jewish prophets and Plato. Its essential conclusions about the nature of Jesus, the resurrection, and sin and redemption are similar to the ideas Nast had expressed dozens of times, and one wonders why he thought it worth while to produce still another edition on the same familiar themes.

In 1883, Walden and Stowe of Cincinnati printed Nast's *Das biblische Christenthum und seine Gegensätze* (Biblical Christianity and Its Opposition), as a book of 256 pages. It was largely derived from the works of distinguished theologians, and the introduction was taken from a study which an evangelical pastor in Canada, Rev. William Kloeti, had sent Nast for publication. In each chapter Nast acknowledges his indebtedness to his sources.

The work is a curious miscellany. There are chapters on the angels, God's plans for mankind, the problem of evil, conscience, and time and eternity, and the book ends with a chapter on "The Heaven of the Naturalist." The book is another vigorous protest against agnosticism, rationalism, deism, materialism and pantheism, and a plea to return to a simple Christian faith. Nast castigated the German freethinkers, humanism, "the anti-Christian Jewish press of Germany," and the American public schools for their indifference to religion. He had sincere praise for Kant, but Schelling, Fichte and Hegel he accused of destroying men's religions. He disliked Darwin; he repeated his strictures about the "dead orthodoxies" of Roman Catholicism, a "skeleton without a spirit"; he chided the Protestants for their denominational quarrelling and denounced the use of church buildings for profane purposes, such as church bazaars. The book pleads for the preservation of Christian culture and maintains that Christianity has freed the slaves, given aid to the poor and oppressed, raised the status of women, blessed the world with some of its greatest art, and guaranteed freedom of conscience.

Part II contains a curious chapter on the nature of the angels. They are "children of God," have bodies, but are freed from all the conditions that circumscribe life on earth, including sex. They live near the throne of the Heavenly Father, and some rise in the angelic hierarchy, with Michael and Gabriel at the very top, to become "holy angels." In other chapters, the book deals with the creation, man's human and spiritual characteristics, free will and salvation. The problem of evil is traced to selfishness, which started with Adam and Eve, when Eve was the doubter, and Adam had to be tried in order to develop freedom of choice. In his quotations and citations, Nast revealed his usual familiarity with ancient and modern literature. Among many others, he referred to Pascal, Juvenal, Pliny, Horace and Cicero, among the ancients, and to such moderns as the German philosophers, Goethe, and England's Admiral Nelson.

Was ist und will der Methodismus? (What is Methodism and What Does It Want?) is one of Nast's smaller works. It appeared first in the form of material for the *Apologete* and several tracts. In 1853, the various essays were brought together in a small book, but each essay is paged separately. Nast's thesis is that the Methodist church is the true church of Christ. This having been settled, he deals with such practical matters as class and weekly experience meetings, group prayer, camp meetings, the circuit rider system, and miscellaneous advice to church members. There also are essays on sin, repentance and forgiveness; and a dialogue on "Why have you abandoned the faith?" The final article is taken from John Wesley, to prove that "Methodism is nothing else but the religion of the Bible."

Nast's *The Gospel Records: Their Genuineness, Authenticity, Historic Variety, and Inspiration, with some Preliminary Remarks on the Gospel History*, appeared as a 373-page book in 1866. It is essentially a rearrangement and repetition of Nast's views as originally expounded in the *Apologete* and earlier books. In the introduction, he points out proudly that his work was endorsed by the Board of Methodist Bishops as a guide for ministerial study and already had been adopted as a text in several schools. Nast undertook once more to prove from historical records, the Gospels, and the early evangelists who saw and heard him, that Jesus was an historical personality. He admits, however, that no existing manuscripts of the New Testament can be traced farther back than the fourth century.

In 1866, the Methodist Publishing House published a book of 128 pages entitled *Der hundertjährige Bestand des amerikanischen Methodismus* (the Hundreth Anniversary of American Methodism). Nast's contribution ran to nearly seventy pages, in the form of a lecture, in German, in which he reviewed the history of Methodism from Wesley, Whitefield and Asbury to the present and proclaimed the Methodist church as the true apostolic church. In a somewhat shorter contribution, Heinrich Liebhart reviewed the role of Methodism in higher learning.

Nast also was associated in an editorial capacity with the preparation of hymnals, catechisms and other manuals of German Methodism. In 1839, in collaboration with Peter Schmucker, he edited a book of worship of 451 pages which included 369 songs selected from German and English hymnals, here and abroad. Nast chose the texts and Schmucker the melodies. Other German Methodist hymnals appeared in 1865 and 1888, and were built largely on this earlier collection.

Nast's catechisms began to appear in 1868. They were based largely on Dr. Philip Schaff's *Christliche Katechismus* (Christian Catechism), from which whole passages were lifted. On October 5, 1868, the *Apologete* announced a "new catechism" of 156 pages, by the editor. In the various sections, Nast deals in order with the Trinity, creation, divine law, Jesus, the Holy Spirit, the church, the way of salvation, death, resurrection and the Last Judgment.[16] An enlarged English edition appeared in 1869, intended for older children and as a text for teachers of the smaller catechism.

To the end of his days, Nast was busy with new projects for publication. On several occasions, articles from the *Apologete* were reissued, in bound form, at nominal cost. The twenty-four page brochure, *What is a Spirit?* was available for three cents a copy. In 1878, it was reported that Nast was working in Berea on a history of German missions, but the project was never completed.

From a lifetime of prodigious study, research and writing, Nast undoubtedly would have selected his *Commentary on the New Testament* as his *magnum opus*. The *Commentary*, in German, was authorized by the Methodist General Conference as early as 1852, and in 1859 Nast was provided with an assistant to speed the project. In the same year, the *Apologete* announced that the editor would have to reduce his preaching assignments, especially dedicatory sermons for new churches, in order to devote more time to research. Nast explained that he would have to consult all the older English and German works on theology and the new works on exegesis. Before long, he began publishing his findings in the *Apologete*, and must have bored many of his readers with his elaborate footnotes and definition of terms. The *Commentary* was first sold in installments, as they appeared in the *Apologete*. The first four numbers, of sixty-four pages each, sold for thirty cents a number. Nast estimated that his finished work would embrace from thirty to thirty-six such pieces and would cost about $9.

In the *Apologete* of April 19, 1860, Nast published his bibliography for the *Commentary*. It included twenty-one German and twenty English titles. Among German sources, he listed Rudolf Stier's eight-volume *Die Reden des Herrn Jesu*, and other books on the New Testament and homiletics, by Hermann Olshausen, J. P. Lange, F. A. Tholuk, Heinrich A. W. Meyer, Johann A. Bengel, H. L. Heubner, Otto von Gerlach, and Heinrich Richter. From English sources, besides Wesley's *Notes on the New Testament*, he relied on commentaries by A. Clark, Joseph Benson, Joseph Sutcliffe, Matthew Henry, R. Watson, Philip Doddridge and a half dozen others.

Nast frankly admitted that " if no copyright was infringed thereby," he appropriated entire sections from his sources, although he always gave credit in his footnotes. Despite this practice, Nast's *Commentary* is more than a mere compilation of other writers' books. He stated his own opinions on many points and thought he was quite original in his treatment of the twenty-fourth chapter of Matthew. He introduced foreign scholars whose work had not been published in the United States and tried to write a strictly historical narrative, unhampered by narrow dogmatism. The *Commentary* contains many Greek and Latin terms, quotations from the early church fathers, from historians like Tacitus and Josephus, and from such modern writers as Grotius, Mill, Hume and

Schaff. Nast believed his work would attract the laity, as well as the ministers, but above all, he hoped to provide another antidote for the poison of rationalism and make his book a bulwark of the faith against the attacks of science upon revelation. Nast never really finished his task. In 1880, he was working in Berea on the Gospel of John. In 1882, he and his son Albert were involved in a discussion of what could be said about the wedding of Cana, whether the wine was intoxicating and how long it had been allowed to ferment. As late as 1894, while in retirement in Lakeside, Ohio, Nast was still working on the Epistles of Paul.

The first German edition of the *Commentary* was issued simultaneously in Cincinnati and Bremen, in 1860.[17] From then on, Nast plodded along, from Gospel to Gospel, and in 1865, his commentary on Matthew and Mark, a tome of 760 pages, appeared in English, from the press of Poe and Hitchcock in Cincinnati. The English edition was shorter than the German, contained fewer homiletical suggestions, and was dedicated to Rev. Adam Poe, D. D., "under whose ministry the author was brought into the Liberty of the Gospel." Nast had engaged a translator but was so disappointed with his work that he had " to think the whole work over in English."

In a 150-page introduction, Nast again belabored the genuineness of the New Testament texts and the credibility of their authors. He saw no more reason to challenge the authorship of the books of the Bible than to question Xenophon's *Anabasis* or Suetonius' *Life of the Caesars*. He devoted a section to the disastrous results of the "higher criticism," and another to the state of the world among the Jews, Greeks and Romans when Jesus arrived on earth. He followed Christ's life in detail, accepted all the miracles and the bodily resurrection, explained the parables, and devoted eleven pages to the pros and cons of infant baptism, which he thought the New Testament neither commands nor prohibits. Most of his homiletical suggestions were drawn from the English periodical *The Homilist.*

It is interesting to observe that in all this theological detail there is little reference to the social gospel, for Nast was completely absorbed in the problem of individual salvation. One exception can be found in the homiletical suggestions in the English edition,[18] where Nast pointed out that Jesus instructed his apostles to attend to the material as well as the spiritual needs of mankind and "give bread to the hungry as well as Bibles to the ignorant." He charged the church with neglecting its duties as a "secular benefactor" and "a genial messenger of deep and genuine philanthropy." The other exception is his reference to the passage to render unto Caesar the things that are Caesar's. Here Nast argued that "absolutistic principles were neither taught by Christ nor by his apostles" and that Christianity is not at war with democracy, and at this point, he interpolated long passages from the American Declaration of Independence.[19]

The reviews of the *Commentary* were generally favorable and Nast was justly proud of his work. A reviewer in *The Methodist Quarterly Review* of 1864 commented on Nast's learning, industry and remarkable bilingualism and recommended his work as "a thesaurus for the lay reader, for the family and for the minister." Nevertheless, this particular reviewer, more fundamentalist even than Nast, took issue on some theological points and apparently was disturbed by the author's scholarly, historical approach, which he thought deprived the discourse of all value as "a prophecy against skepticism, furnishing the basis of modern Universalism, and destroying the scripture proof of a future literal judgment day."

Nast had suggested that the "theory of verbal inspiration" was not essential to the belief that the Gospel records were a divine revelation and rested upon divine authority.[20] Four years later, W. F. Warren, professor in the Methodist Theological Institute of Boston and later president of Boston University, wrote another review for the same journal. He lauded Nast's scholarship and thought the *Commentary* was the best of its kind produced on this continent and that the English edition was superior to the German. Moreover, Warren was satisfied that Nast had provided an excellent antidote "to meet the difficulties of modern skepticism," with "special attention to the cavils and sophisms of current infidelity." [21]

To what extent Nast's *Commentary* is still useful in Methodist theological circles it is difficult to ascertain, but it remains as a literary monument to an indefatigable scholar, trained in the best German tradition, who remained at his books to his dying day. The layman will be impressed with the scholarly apparatus of the *Commentary*, but can hardly regard it as anything but very difficult reading.

As early as 1878, the *Apologete* carried a notice that the patriarch of German Methodism was in Berea, working on his autobiography, and in the early 1880's, Nast seriously considered writing the story of his life. His son in 1882 urged him to preserve all the letters from prominent church leaders, because "they may be of considerable interest and value hereafter in tracing the history of your life and work." Nast thought it might be his duty to write the story of his divinely commissioned task to preach Methodism to the Germans. In 1887, he announced he was at work on the autobiography, and on December 16 of that year, his old friend Adam Miller, preacher, publisher and medical practitioner, wrote him from Chicago to say that all his plans for another volume on the history of the German missions, in which Nast would have figured prominently, had gone awry, because Nast had announced his intention to tell his own story. Every German minister would have subscribed for Miller's book, but if Nast wrote his autobiography, Miller thought he would not find a single purchaser. Miller concealed his pecuniary interest in the matter by insisting that Nast was too modest to tell the real story, whereas Miller would have written with a memory still "fresh and strong." There was no reason for concern, however. If Nast ever started an autobiography, it is certain that he never proceeded far with it and probably the whole project died in the planning stage.

12

CARRYING THE GOSPEL TO GERMANY

Not long after Nast began his mission to the Germans in the United States, his thoughts turned to ways and means of exporting Methodism to the German-speaking areas of Europe. The missions founded in the United States prospered so well that as early as 1844 the Methodist General Conference entertained proposals to carry the gospel to Germany, and voted to send Nast to Europe to study the situation first hand and make recommendations for the spread of German Methodism on the Continent.

In 1738, John Wesley had spent nearly three months in the German states and encountered the Moravians, whose faith and practices proved so important in the development of Methodist theology and church polity. The first official Methodist missionary to the Germans was Christopher Gottlieb Müller, a journeyman butcher of Winnenden, Germany, who had gone to England in 1805 to escape military service in the army of Napoleon. In London, Müller was converted to Methodism and licensed as a local preacher by the Wesleyans. In 1830, he spent a short time in Germany organizing Methodist classes and teaching Sunday school in his father's home, a regular meeting place for Moravian pietists in the neighborhood. He returned to England and shortly thereafter was appointed Methodist missionary to Germany. Although he met with opposition from the state church in Württemberg and from pietists who disagreed with him on theological niceties, Müller travelled from village to village, and spread the Methodist gospel so effectively that after eight years of labor, he could claim about six hundred members for his church. When he died in 1858, the London Wesleyans appointed another missionary to continue the work he had begun among his fellow Württembergers.

Germans who had settled in the United States wrote home to friends and relatives of their satisfying religious experiences in Methodist meetings, and their reports helped stimulate a demand from German communities for missionaries who could introduce and develop this particular variety of Protestantism in the fatherland.[1] For a number of years, however, Methodist activities in Germany remained under the supervision of the Wesleyan Missionary Society of London as Methodism gradually spread from its early beginnings in Württemberg to other parts of Germany.

In 1844, the General Conference of the American Methodist church, the last to convene before Methodism split over the slavery issue into a church north and a church south, authorized Nast to go to Germany to report on the opportunities for missionary work on the Continent. Nast arrived in London on August 30, 1844. He experienced some embarrassment when his baggage, opened for customs inspection, was found to contain books published in the United States on which there was a British copyright. In a sermon delivered at Portsmouth he reported on his work in the United States, and in London he attended the meetings of several Methodist missions and discussed plans with prominent British Methodists to translate Fletcher's *Appeal* for a German edition and apparently was assured financial support for the project from English Methodists.

From London, he proceeded to Germany, by way of Rotterdam, and on to Württemberg, his native land. On Christmas, he preached near Stuttgart and administered communion to a little band of worshippers. For watchnight and New Year's Day services, he was in Winnenden, the center of Müller's activities. He preached in several towns and villages in Württemberg, often in the crowded rooms of private homes, and on one occasion, his religious fervor held his congregation so spellbound that he had to order them to disband lest they come in conflict with the police regulations limiting the time of public gatherings. He went on to preach at the mission in Hedelfingen. In Esslingen, he addressed a group of women in a private home and spoke in a schoolroom maintained by a group of pietists. In general, he received a hearty welcome from the latter group, particularly among the " Michelianer," followers of Michael Hahn, a German peasant and theosophist who died in 1819. On two occasions, he spoke from the pulpit of churches where former schoolmates were the ministers. He also handed out Methodist literature, and before long colporteurs were distributing Methodist tracts in several areas of Germany and France. Nast had a most satisfying experience during the first of three visits which he made during his lifetime to the homeland. He visited old friends and relatives and returned to the United States firmly convinced that it was the Lord's will to import Methodism into Germany and that it would reap a bountiful harvest there.[2]

His favorable report was supported by requests for Methodist missionaries which came from Germany. The German revolution of 1848 contributed to the eagerness of German Methodists in the United States to launch their work on the Continent, for they believed that the upheaval guaranteed a larger measure of religious freedom and weakened the position of the Lutheran church in a number of the German states. Methodists were eager to do their part in rescuing " the German race from unbelief and sin." In 1848, Nast and Jacoby, as delegates to the General Conference in Pittsburgh, stressed the changes which they believed imminent in Germany because of the popular uprising and emphasized the need for immediate support of their missionary project.

In 1849, the General Missionary Committee of the Methodist church officially approved a plan to dispatch German Methodist missionaries to Europe and to send two missionaries to initiate the work in Germany. Ludwig S. Jacoby, one of Nast's earliest converts, who was presiding elder of the Quincy District of the Illinois Conference at the time, received the first appointment. He was followed within the year by Carl Döring and Ludwig Nippert. Bremen, where there was considerable religious freedom, was designated as the headquarters for the activities of the American Methodists in Germany. Since the Wesleyans already were active in southern Germany, the choice of a northerly location seemed practical and wise. In the next forty years, the work begun in 1849 developed into a German Methodist church of some fifteen thousand regular members, sufficient progress to reassure the leaders of American Methodism that their German mission had the blessing of Heaven. They believed that by using Nast and his followers as his instrument, God intended to first save and then use the German nation "for his own all-wise and glorious purposes."

Ludwig Sigmund Jacoby, the first German Methodist missionary from the United States to Germany, was a native of Alt-Strelitz, Mecklenburg, whose parents were Jews. As a boy of fifteen, he had been apprenticed to a merchant in Hamburg and later was a travelling salesman for a commercial house in Leipzig. In 1835, he was baptized by a Lutheran pastor. Three years later, he was in business in England, and in 1839, he came to the United States and settled in Cincinnati. Here he attended Methodist services at Burke Chapel conducted by an uneducated but religiously inspired German who was a convert from Catholicism. Jacoby heard Nast preach and was so impressed that he began attending Methodist class meetings and prayer meetings. In due course, he was converted, and published an appeal in Nast's *Apologete* to his German fellow countrymen to follow his example. Three months later, Jacoby was a licensed local preacher, distributing Methodist tracts among German laborers working on the Ohio canal.

In 1841, he was assigned the difficult task of evangelizing the "godless" Germans of St. Louis. In his new field of operations, he made the customary house-to-house visits to distribute Methodist literature, preached wherever he could find a room and a handful of listeners, and suffered the usual ridicule and hostility which a certain class of Germans reserved for "fanatical Methodists."[3] In 1842, when the cornerstone was laid for his first little church, several Germans poured a pitcher of whiskey over the stone. He rode a large circuit in Illinois and Missouri, and in 1844, became the presiding elder of the newly organized district of Quincy, Illinois. On October 20, 1849, at the age of thirty-six, and much against the wishes of his wife, he sailed for his new post in Bremen, armed with little except enthusiasm and five dollars' worth of Methodist tracts. On December 23, 1849, he preached his first sermon in a rented hall in a village some twenty miles from Bremen, to some four hundred listeners interested in the new gospel of salvation. He spent twenty-two years in Germany. He returned to the United States in 1871, and two years later was made presiding elder of the Illinois District. In the course of his long career in the United States and Germany he published several books about Methodist theology.

From Bremen the seeds of German Methodism were scattered over the German states by a small but growing band of American Germans whom the church assigned to the German mission field. Their number included such bright stars as Engelhardt Riemenschneider, Ludwig Nippert, Carl Döring, Heinrich Nuelsen and others. Nippert had the longest service in Germany and became the outstanding leader of the German work.

Nippert was brought to the United States from Alsace by his parents in 1830, when he was five years old. He was converted to Methodism in Captina, in Monroe County, Ohio, in 1840, by German preachers active among the Germans in that area. Shortly after his conversion, he went to Cincinnati to learn the printer's trade as an apprentice of the Methodist Book Concern. He affiliated with the German Methodist group, became a class leader at the age of eighteen, and in 1845 was licensed to preach by one of the quarterly meetings in Captina. Nippert also served as a local preacher in Cincinnati and in Louisville and then for a brief period attended Asbury College in Greencastle, Indiana, later known as DePauw University. He directed the mission in Indianapolis, where he sustained himself on a salary of fifty dollars a year and found board and lodging in the homes of sympathetic, English-speaking Methodists. He covered a large circuit in Indiana and like other circuit riders rode through mud and swamp, high water and winter snows, to preach in schoolhouses or private homes. His services to Methodism as the first German missionary in that area eventually were recognized by the dedication of a Nippert Memorial Church in Indianapolis.

After serving several missions in Pennsylvania and Ohio, and riding the large Delaware, Ohio, circuit at a salary of $150 a year, Nippert had made up his mind to join the migration to California in 1850, when he received the call to go to Bremen. He became the most distinguished member of the German Methodist mission in Germany. He was especially interested in building a chapel in Bremen for immigrants and seamen, " to break the bread of life and give help and counsel." [4] He later taught at the Methodist Seminary in Frankfurt, published books on theology and church history, as well as biographies of Asbury and Fletcher, and was a regular contributor to Nast's *Apologete*. Despite his meager formal training, his writings reveal a mastery of German style and a remarkable knowledge of the details of Methodist theology. In the long accounts which he wrote for the *Apologete*, he not only dealt with religious matters but also reported on many facets of European life as he came to understand them from extensive travels in Germany and Switzerland. In 1886, after thirty-six years abroad, he returned to the United States, where he died in 1894.

However heaven-blessed the work in Germany may have

been, the early missionaries from the United States had no easy task. A Methodist was still a curiosity in Germany, and many people came to Methodist meetings to scoff and not to pray or simply because they wanted to find out what this curious sect was like. The Lutheran state churches, with few exceptions, were hostile to what they considered another divisive force in the world of Protestantism and, at best, regarded Methodism as but another "experimental religion" which was undermining the fruits of the Reformation. The temporal authorities in many German states were equally hostile, and Jacoby, Nippert and other early Methodist missionaries encountered ridicule and even abuse in a number of localities where they tried to preach, were harassed by local magistrates and the police, and fined for preaching in unauthorized public assemblies. Many who came to their meetings refused to remove their hats, even for prayer, interrupted and yelled at the speakers, smoked cigars and brought barking dogs along to molest the preachers.

Saxony was especially hostile to Methodists and kept Methodist preachers under police surveillance, and they were required to clear the title of their sermons in advance with the authorities. A bitter controversy raged in Saxony and several smaller states over whether Methodists could be buried in cemeteries controlled by the local pastors, and special regulations were made to govern marriage ceremonies and baptisms performed by Methodist ministers. Erhard Wunderlich, an early missionary in Saxony, was fined several times for unauthorized preaching and, on one occasion, spent several weeks in jail.[5] In 1850, the Bremen police, assigned to give Carl Döring protection, were unable to prevent a mob from throwing stones into the hall where he was trying to make himself heard. Neighbors often complained to the authorities that the Methodists were disturbing the peace with their loud singing and praying, and occasionally Lutheran ministers published violent attacks on the Methodists in local newspapers.[6] Nippert reported to Nast from Heilbronn in 1852 that he had been denied the use of all churches and had been forced to preach in private homes, in schoolhouses, in barns where animal noises interrupted his sermons, and in the open air, when weather permitted. On many occasions, he was spied upon by the police.[7] In Hesse, where the government was battling both rationalists and pietists, Engelhardt Riemenschneider was refused a permit to speak,[8] and he encountered similar opposition from the local officials of Lauterbach and Frankfurt.[9] Gendarmes frequently interrupted Methodist meetings by demanding the preacher's passport or confiscated the tracts which he tried to distribute.

Nippert was forbidden to work in Hanover and Brunswick, but Magdeburg allowed him to preach without surveillance and to advertise his meetings in the newspapers. In other localities he was menaced by yelling crowds who threw stones and tore his coat, while the police stood idly by. As late as 1878, an eager gendarme in a little village of Hesse tried to keep Nippert from preaching.[10] Jacoby thought such disorderly outbursts were sometimes encouraged by Lutheran and Evangelical pastors, and by local newspaper owners and tavern keepers.[11] Conditions were hardly better in Switzerland when German missionaries moved into that little country. In Canton Bern, the owner of a home was fined for letting a Methodist preach on the premises, and the use of the workers' hall was denied to the missionaries. At least one German missionary concluded that as far as freedom to preach the Methodist gospel was concerned, conditions were worse in democratic Switzerland than in monarchical Germany.[12]

Undeterred by the ridicule and open hostility which they encountered in many parts of Germany, the American missionaries would not be silenced, for they were sure that they were doing the Lord's work. Their staff was slowly augmented by new arrivals from the United States and by a few local recruits. By 1850, Jacoby had a Methodist class of twenty-two in Bremen, and before the end of the year, several hundred children were enrolled in his Sunday school classes. Döring and Nippert arrived in the spring of 1850, and in the summer, Eberhardt Wunderlich, a German immigrant who had been converted in the United States, returned to begin missionary activities in Sachsen-Weimar. In 1851, Nippert was transferred to Württemberg, and Heinrich Nuelsen came to Bremen to work among the emigrants and to begin a distinguished career abroad.

In 1850, the German group began publishing the *Evangelist* in Bremen, as a counterpart to Nast's American *Apologete*. The project was supported by an initial subsidy from Charles and Henry Baker of Baltimore. Four years later, the *Kinderfreund* was launched in Bremen as a companion publication for younger people. By 1860, German Methodists had a flourishing printing establishment in Bremen, and a steady flow of tracts, brochures and books poured from its presses. Jacoby, the first superintendent of the German work in the fatherland, by 1856 had a staff of five missionaries, twelve helpers, four colporteurs and three clerks, and by that time conferences of German Methodist preachers and missionaries in Germany had become a regular procedure.[18] Ten years later, a lively Methodist revival was in progress on the Frisian Islands, off the coast of Schleswig.

In 1875, many of Sankey's gospel hymns were translated and published in a German edition, edited by E. Geb-

hart, "the German Sankey," under the title of *Frohe Bot-
schaft*. By the 1890's, German Methodism had spread widely
in Germany; into Switzerland, where a separate German Conference was formed in 1887; and into Austria-Hungary; and
at least one Methodist missionary tour had been made in
Russia. In 1891, Germany had 72 German Methodist preachers and 10,580 members, and Switzerland claimed a membership of 5307. The *Evangelist* had a circulation of 13,500
and the *Kinderfreund* 19,800, and the Methodist Deaconess
Homes flourished in Berlin, Breslau and Dresden.[14] By 1925,
and despite the ravages of World War I, a Central Conference
for Mid-Europe, called by Bishop Nuelsen from his headquarters in Zurich, attracted delegates from eight Conferences,
from North Germany and South Germany, Switzerland,
Austria, Hungary, Bulgaria, Jugoslavia and Russia.

Nast followed the development of the work which
stemmed from his pioneering efforts in Cincinnati with great
satisfaction and pride. He kept up a steady correspondence
with the leaders of the various "mission stations" in Europe,
reported their activities in detail in the *Apologete*, and appealed for additional financial support. His communications
with Jacoby, Nippert and others kept him in touch with the
leading church publications on the Continent, especially with
new books in the field of theology. Many English-speaking
Methodists in the United States were deeply interested in
this revival of "primitive Methodism" through the zeal and
devotion of the German Methodists and were especially happy
to note the conversion of hundreds in Germany "from the
errors of Romanism."[15]

Less than ten years after the German Methodists began
their campaign to evangelize Germany, they planned to found
a mission institute to train young Germans as missionaries

to their own people. Their educational enterprise was launched in 1858, with the opening of a school in Bremen, with three students in attendance and a faculty which consisted of Nippert as director and professor of theology, Jacoby and W. Schwarz. Classes were held in the attic of a preacher's residence. Students had to be at least twenty years old and were required to do manual labor four hours a day to help meet the costs of their education. The constitution and by-laws for the institute, drawn by Nippert, Jacoby and Döring, prescribed a rigid schedule of activities. Students were expected to arise at five in the morning, clean their rooms, and be ready for Bible reading at seven. They sang, prayed and studied together until nine, when their teacher arrived and began formal instruction. Classes met from nine to eleven. The next hour was devoted to quizzing the students in the catechism and church discipline. The curriculum, in which English was a required subject, was based on the philosophy that "the heart made the theolog." Every afternoon, except Saturday, was devoted to manual labor, usually in the Methodist publishing house in Bremen. The evenings were filled with study or religious meetings, and on Sunday, students did field work in the Methodist missions in and around Bremen.[16] Shortly after its establishment, Jacoby assumed the directorship of the little institute, and the school was moved into its own house in 1860. In 1861, William F. Warren, later president of Boston University, joined the teaching staff and subsequently wrote two textbooks for the school, one in theology and one in logic. From 1861 to 1866, before the institute was moved from Bremen, the institute prepared twenty-nine young Germans for the Methodist ministry.

In 1866, John T. Martin, a native of Baltimore, gave

$25,000 to move the school and establish the Martin Mission-
ary Institute in Frankfurt-am-Main. Martin had been born
an Episcopalian but was converted to Methodism at the age
of sixteen. He became a successful businessman in St. Louis,
and here he met Jacoby in 1841. During the Civil War,
Martin had contracts with the government, which ran into
millions, to furnish clothing for the army, and Jacoby appealed to him to use some of his profits from the war for the
support of the German Methodist program in Germany.
Martin responded with what was considered a very generous
gift of 100,000 German marks for the development of the
training school.

The Martin Missionary Institute was opened in Frankfurt in 1869, with Nippert as director. It grew slowly, and
in 1871, partly because of the effects of the Franco-German
War, had only eleven students. Six years later, the student
body had increased by only one. The same rigid program of
study and religious exercises initiated at Bremen was continued
in Frankfurt. The day's activities began at five in the morning and continued to ten at night, and all students were
expected to do field work. In 1871, Jacoby invited Nast to
join the faculty of the Frankfurt school, but because Mrs.
Nast strongly objected to living in Germany, Nast declined.
In 1914, when World War I broke out, the Institute was
located on a new campus, and its facilities were used by the
government as an army hospital. At the time, the enrollment
totalled forty students, including three from Russia and two
women who were preparing for missionary work. Despite
the relatively small student body throughout its history, the
school at Frankfurt trained a number of outstanding Methodist leaders and had several outstanding people on its faculty.
These included William F. Warren of Boston University,

John F. Hurst, who went to Drew University in New Jersey to become professor, president and a bishop, and several members of the faculty of Baldwin-Wallace College in Ohio.[17]

Nast, recognized as the father of an international German Methodist movement, made two additional visits to the fatherland, to see with his own eyes what his followers had been able to accomplish. In 1857, he went as a delegate to the Evangelical Alliance meeting in Berlin, where his primary function was to tell the story of Methodism as it had developed in the United States. Mrs. Nast accompanied him, and it was at this time that they put their son Albert, then a lad of eleven, in a school at Kornthal, in Württemberg, operated by a relative who had been converted to Methodism, where in a proper religious environment, the boy could get a thorough German elementary education.

Nast reported in detail to readers of the *Apologete* about his experiences in Germany and was careful to explain that he paid the expenses of his family out of his own meager resources. When he arrived in Bremen, Nippert, Jacoby, Döring and Riemenschneider were on hand to greet him. He inspected the Methodist publishing house and preached in several churches to audiences which included a number of emigrants on their way to America. In Berlin, he made a long address to the Evangelical Conference, calling for greater unity among Protestant groups and stressing the emphasis Protestantism, in contrast with Catholicism, put on religious freedom. The Conference met in the old Garrison Church in Berlin, with 1254 delegates from Germany, France, Great Britain, Austria, Denmark and America in attendance. German and English were the languages of procedure. The proceedings opened with a magnificent rendition of Mendelssohn's " One Hundredth Psalm " by the royal cathedral choir.

Church leaders from various countries and Protestant faiths discussed a number of theological questions, including the special problems which Protestant churches encountered in Roman Catholic countries. Nast distributed Methodist literature among the delegates and spoke for an hour on American Methodism, stressing the "moral and religious destitution" of the German element in the United States because of the inroads of Romanism and rationalism. He explained the cardinal doctrines of Methodism and described the structure and polity of the Methodist church and defended such Methodist institutions as the "mourners' bench" and other emotional features of Methodist procedures in terms which must have sounded somewhat strange to the ears of many European theologians.[18]

During his sojourn in Germany in 1857, Nast visited Oldenburg, Frankfurt and several other cities and preached in a number of them; attended the quarterly meeting in Heilbronn; visited with family and friends in Stuttgart; and renewed his contacts with companions of his student days. His letters to the *Apologete* indicate that he was deeply moved by his experiences in Germany, and particularly, by his return to his native Württemberg.[19]

Twenty years later, in 1877, when he was in his seventieth year, he visited Germany for the last time. Meantime, the German Methodist church in the United States had grown to over forty thousand members, with nearly six hundred ministers, and there were ten thousand members and seventy-seven ministers in Germany. When Nast left Cincinnati, the Race Street congregation gave him a warm farewell. In a letter to his son Albert, he expressed disappointment that only one German minister had come to the boat in New York to see him off and that he was not invited to sit at the captain's table. On shipboard, he distributed copies of the *Apologete* among passengers and crew.

Nast preached in Berlin, Bremen, Frankfurt, Cologne, and other German cities and attended Methodist conferences in several places. He stopped for a week in Kornthal, on his way to Switzerland, and the church choir sang a number especially composed in his honor. In Stuttgart, he was invited to preach in the great concert hall. In Switzerland, he participated in Methodist meetings in Basel, Schaffhausen, Zurich and other cities but was disappointed to find "great jealousy at every effort of a foreign church or nationality to introduce their mode of thinking and church work." [20]

After finishing his tour of duty for the Methodist cause, he returned to his beloved Württemberg to spend more time with relatives and then went to the Black Forest for a rest cure. He refused to attend the four hundredth anniversary of the University of Tübingen and, in a letter to his wife, described the festivities as "a scandal to a civilized Christian country—a great carnival of drinking and carousing." [21] Like many other German immigrants who returned to the fatherland after many years in the United States only to find that they no longer felt at home in Germany, Nast was eager to return to America. He had been homesick for his family and American friends from the day he had left New York. He wrote his wife almost daily, sometimes both before and after breakfast, and begged for more letters from home. He enjoyed many pleasant occasions during his final visit to Germany, but his roots were now so deeply fixed in American soil that he could no longer feel at home anywhere else.

13

THE NAST FAMILY

$\mathcal{A}$s a general rule, ministers were expected to marry and have families fairly early in their career, and we may be sure that Nast weighed his responsibilities in this direction as seriously as he did the other obligations of a ministerial career. His first years in America had been difficult years, marked by a prolonged inner struggle for salvation and complicated by his romantic experience with the widow of Duncan's Island, but by the time he began his missionary work among the Ohio Germans, both issues had been settled. He was sure God had chosen him for the Methodist ministry, and he had reached an age when young men were expected to marry. His elders in the ministry not only advised him to consider matrimony but were prepared to suggest eligible young ladies from among their congregations.

Long courtships, or even much acquaintance, were not

regarded at the time as special prerequisites for a successful marriage. Sometimes the matter was settled by correspondence, with ministers acting as intermediaries, and it is surprising how often the advice of preachers was accepted without serious questioning. In his later years, as the revered patriarch of his church, Nast himself arranged several marriages for colleagues in the ministry and still more for members of his flock. German Methodist weddings were rather austere occasions. Very often the bride had neither veil nor ring. An hour of prayer generally preceded the ceremony, which was followed by a social occasion marked by nothing more stimulating than lemonade and sweets for the wedding party. Though there was little romance, as judged by modern standards, many of these marriages, entered into without benefit of marriage counsellors, seem to have lasted a lifetime, without serious trouble or complications, and with a reasonable measure of mutual satisfaction.

The woman whom young Nast chose for his partner through life was quite different in temperament and background from the pious, serious, introspective and somewhat morose young German who led her to the altar. Their courtship lacked the romance that had marked Nast's sojourn on Duncan's Island, but the union turned out to be a stable and generally satisfactory relationship, based on mutual respect, affection and tolerance, and it endured for sixty-two years.

Margaret Eliza McDowell, to whom Nast addressed his suit, was born in 1815 in Fulton, Ohio, now a part of greater Cincinnati. She was of Scotch Highland stock, and her people had settled in Pennsylvania before the Revolution. Her father was Joseph McDowell. He married Martha Steele, in Yorktown, Pennsylvania, and the couple came to Ohio in 1806 to farm a small piece of land in Fulton which sloped

down to the Ohio River. Eliza's father died in 1863, at the
age of eighty-three; her mother died while she was still a
young girl. Over the grave in a cemetery in the east end
of Cincinnati, where the father lies buried, there is the
inscription,

> Farewell, my friends and children dear.
> I am not dead, but sleeping here.
> My debts are paid, my grave you see,
> Prepare for death—it soon could be.

Eliza McDowell was born a Scotch Presbyterian, thoroughly instructed in the Bible, and reared according to strict
Sabbatarian principles. She could recite from memory many
church hymns and long passages from the Holy Scriptures.
Before she met her future husband, she had become a Methodist, probably because she lived for a time with a devout
Methodist seamstress who taught her Wesley's hymns as well
as how to sew. Eliza attended Methodist class meetings and
taught Sunday school in Cincinnati, and later, was especially
interested in foreign missions. She met Nast when she was
twenty years old.

Descriptions and photographs of Eliza McDowell indicate that as a young woman she was tall, straight and good
looking, with coal-black eyes, and hair parted precisely in
the middle. She had a sunny disposition, and was full of
energy and enthusiasm. She was a good hymn singer and a
devout believer in the efficacy of prayer for all occasions. But
she was frequently criticised by her more rigid fellow Methodists for wearing a silver buckle on her belt and ribbons in
her hair, adornments of the human frame of which both
Calvinists and Methodists disapproved as sinful. According
to a family legend, Nast first called on the young lady to

reason with her about the frivolity of wearing gay ribbons on her bonnet.

Adam Miller, one of the earliest German Methodist preachers, who never suffered from undue modesty and who had helped Nast during his struggles for salvation, claimed credit for directing young Nast's attention to Eliza, but there is no way to prove or disprove the story. In any case, on June 21, 1836, after about a year's acquaintance, Nast wrote the young lady a proposal, addressed to "Dear Sister." He explained that after long hours of prayer over the matter, he had finally concluded that he "would be much more happy and useful" if he could find a partner for "life's uneven journey." He went on to say that he had no worldly goods and that his poorly paid vocation would make it impossible to establish a family for at least two years, but he added, "Love is strong and inventive and if joined with confidence in the kind providence of God could easily leap over the wall of poverty." Since he had not yet been regularly ordained, he would have to seek the permission of his elders in the ministry to marry, but he wanted to have the matter settled before he left Cincinnati to ride the Ohio circuit. He begged Eliza to "ask the Lord for direction" and let him know whether she would approve "a more intimate acquaintance." The letter was signed "your affectionate and respectful friend." On August 1, 1836, the couple were married by Rev. Granville Moody of Fulton.

During the first year of her marriage, the bride taught school as a member of the teaching staff of the female seminary in Worthington, Ohio, to supplement her circuit rider husband's salary of $100 a year. Nast could visit his young wife only every six weeks, when his missionary duties brought him into central Ohio. There were twenty-four young ladies in

the Worthington Seminary, and they were to be instructed in a
full curriculum which included mathematics, rhetoric, history,
geography, philosophy and theology, as well as other " common
things." Judging from Eliza's lack of formal schooling, we
may assume that " common things " received more attention
than more formal subjects, but Mrs. Nast seems to have been
successful with her young charges. When she resigned, one
of the girls presented her with a poem, entitled " The Parting,"
which read:

> To say adieu excites a tear
> When from a friend to sever
> 'Tis hard to part, when harboring fear
> Whispers, we part forever.
> Eliza when rolling years have intervened
> And new formed friends engage your thoughts,
> This little scrole [sic] perhaps if seen
> May call to mind a friend forgot.

Before long, the young couple were able to establish
residence in Cincinnati, and Eliza wrote her sister that her
husband's " gloominess is wearing off." Mrs. Nast proved to
be a good cook and seamstress, and a thrifty, even parsimoni-
ous, housekeeper. She made her husband's shirts and did
plain and fancy sewing. Though their resources were meager,
they gave shelter to many people in their home, and they
took in to live with them two daughters of a friend of Mrs.
Nast. Their most distinguished charge, however, was Charles
Nordhoff author of *Politics for Young Americans*. When his
father died, young Nordhoff was entrusted to Nast and
worked as a printer's devil on the *Apologete*. Nast urged
him to develop his talent for writing, and Nordhoff became
the author of several books, worked for Harper and Brothers,

edited the New York *Evening Post,* and was Washington correspondent for the New York *Herald.* His circle of friends included such distinguished Americans as Carl Schurz, Henry Adams and Abram S. Hewitt. Nordhoff never forgot his indebtedness to Nast, corresponded frequently with him, and on several occasions was able to be helpful with family problems.

The long years the Nasts lived together were not without their problems, and each had to make concessions to the other, for they were different in background, tastes and temperament. As she grew older, Mrs. Nast suffered from sinus, catarrh and increasing deafness and became something of a hypochondriac. She blamed her infirmities on the dirt and climate of Cincinnati, which she hated, and she finally persuaded her husband to move to Berea, though this must have interfered seriously with his editorial duties in Cincinnati. Nast wrote his older son William, " Ma is tired of boarding, but we cannot think of going to housekeeping in or near Cincinnati. Ma cannot enjoy herself in Cincinnati." For considerable periods, after the move to Berea, Nast had to live alone in Cincinnati, in a private home, and get his meals in hotels. This proved expensive, and Nast was frequently in debt and had to borrow to meet his bills. In many of his letters to his children he urged them to be as economical as possible, and as late as 1866, he had to write his son Albert that he was " too poor . . . to send him a Christmas present."

Mrs. Nast was sorely tried by her husband's periods of depression and found it difficult to understand them. When she was in Germany, in 1861, she did not get on with her relatives-in-law, and this, along with her instinctive dislike of Jacoby, caused her husband much embarrassment. He corresponded with his children in English, because " Ma " never completely mastered his native tongue. In 1866, he wrote Albert, "I feel generally, when I leave home, like a man getting up from a meal hungry. . . . I suppose the reason why my children have so little to say to me is because I have been a stranger for so many years." After moving to Berea to satisfy Mrs. Nast, the family alternated for the next twenty years, between Berea and Lakeside, the Methodist summer colony on Lake Erie, and in 1884, they moved to Cincinnati to live at the home of their daughter Fanny in Avondale. They continued to spend their summers at their daughter's cottage in Lakeside.

Whatever misunderstandings and differences of opinion appear in the many letters exchanged between husband and wife during their long lifetime, there can be no doubt about their mutual respect and devotion. Mrs. Nast was genuinely proud of her husband and believed he had qualities which no other Methodist minister had, so that "even strangers learn to respect and love him," and in 1893, in a letter to his daughter Fanny, Nast wrote a moving, affectionate tribute to his wife and companion for more than half a century.

Five children were born to the Nasts over a period of ten years. The first, Ernst Theodore, born July 10, 1838, died early of cholera. His mother was convinced that his death was caused by overdosages of calomel, and thereafter turned to homeopathy, a school of medicine especially popular with German immigrants, including her husband. On June 14, 1840, a second son was born, and named William Frederick. The first girl, Josephine Pulte Nast, arrived in 1842, and derived her middle name from the young homeopath in Cincinnati who was the family doctor at the time. Albert Julius, next in line, was born in 1846. Franzeska Wilhelmina (Fanny) Nast was the last. She was born in 1848, and grew to be more like her mother than any of the other children. She had brown hair, black eyes, and a florid face, and some of her mother's tastes for the beautiful adornments of life of which strict German Methodists disapproved.

By all accounts, William Frederick was a kindly, warm-hearted and generous person, bedevilled throughout his life by an unbridled ambition to make money quickly through business ventures which lacked nothing in imagination but turned out to be utterly impractical. A restless, optimistic, venturesome spirit, he lacked the sound judgment to direct his energies into practical channels, and his life became a tragic record of fantastic schemes which died aborning.

William was devoted to his mother and was obviously her favorite. Toward his father, he was respectful and affectionate, and he tried to understand his religion and his somber attitude toward life, although both were foreign to his nature. Suffering somewhat from delusions of grandeur, he early in life began to pursue material gains which constantly eluded him. His parents worried about the state of his soul, and in their letters begged him to seek salvation. There is no evidence that William ever violated the moral code, although some of his business activities were highly speculative and somewhat peculiar. It must be remembered, however, that he lived in the period after the Civil War when the acquisition and display of worldly goods were regarded as the best evidence of progress, and the nation as a whole was experiencing a moral relapse from the idealism of the war years. Prosperity made many Americans careless about some of the old standards of rectitude.

William received less formal education than any of the other Nast children, simply because his parents at the time could not afford to keep him in school. He went to work as a clerk, and in later years, his parents blamed many of his shortcomings on their failure to provide him with a better education. His mother thought more formal education " would have made a man of him," and wished he might have gone to school in Germany, as his younger brother did. William " makes fun of the Germans," wrote the father in 1859, " but I wish he were more German."

At sixteen, William began working in a Cincinnati bank, but soon gave up the job because he saw no future in it. His father wanted him to learn the printer's trade, but he was not interested. In the fall of 1859, he found employment in New York and was unhappy because, he wrote, he knew so few people there. Nast replied that in Cincinnati he had suffered from too many friends and advised him to make the church and the Sunday school the center of his associations. By 1861, William was back in Cincinnati, working for a railroad and chemical firm.

Apparently young Nast knew how to make the right connections, for in 1861, when Lincoln passed through Cincinnati on his way to Washington for the inauguration, William was one of the reception committee and rode in the parade. When war came the elder Nast urged his son to enlist, and he himself once served briefly in the home guards, but William was angling for a consulship abroad under the new administration. Scores of Germans were clamoring for political rewards for their support of Lincoln in 1860, and many received appointments from the President, who was quite aware of the important role of the German element in the recent elections in the Northwestern states.

It is not altogether clear how young Nast secured his appointment. His father directed him to a friend in the State Department, and to Green Adams, a Kentuckian, who was an auditor in the Treasury. Friends of the Nast family wrote recommendations, and William went to Washington to apply in person. He apparently got no support from Secretary Chase, who knew his father, and he finally had to explain that his family resided in Kentucky, because there were too many applicants from Ohio. He secured a letter of endorsement from the pastor of the Methodist church in Covington. A letter from his father to a friend of William H. Seward, the new Secretary of State, undoubtedly proved helpful. Whatever the exact chain of influence, William was appointed American consul at Stuttgart.

For a young man of twenty-one, the new post proved to be heady wine. Young Nast was eager to break into the court circles of Württemberg, and father Nast soon reproached himself for having helped his son get the appointment. " I am tormented " he wrote, " with the fear that it will be your ruin . . . with your notions of life." The father, moreover, had little respect for the European nobility and warned his son to steer clear of " such empty-headed, hollow-hearted courtiers." Mrs. Nast, in Stuttgart with the children, and therefore able to observe William's activities first hand, was much less critical and was proud of the progress her son was making in Württemberg social circles. She wrote home that William had three suits made in Paris, because he considered German tailors inferior craftsmen,—and one was " a court suit, hat and sword." " European life has a charm for him," observed the proud mother, " which he has inherited from me." She pointed out that William was going to the opera in Stuttgart, and working hard to break into the diplomatic circle, and she thought two things would help him succeed, his handsome appearance and his ability to speak French. The young consul entertained William Dean Howells, when the

latter passed through Stuttgart on his way to a consular post
in Venice, his reward for writing a campaign biography of
Lincoln. William began smoking a Meerschaum pipe; he
grew whiskers to disguise his youth and had himself photo-
graphed in his " court suit." He had little time for his father's
relatives who lived in the area and wrote disparagingly about
them. In the spring of 1862, he made a trip to Munich to
visit Catholic churches at Easter time.

Although he had to do business with them, William
never liked the Germans, and he was particularly angry when
some of them voiced pro-Southern sympathies during the
Civil War. In March, 1862, he hired a detective to track
down a Confederate agent who was buying supplies in
Europe, and he reported the incident at length to Washington.
By this time, however, he was beginning to be bored by some
of his consular duties and considered the post too restricted
for his talents. His salary was a $1,000 a year, and he began
to live beyond his means probably because he thought he was
raising the importance of his consular post by indulging in
greater social activities. He sent his father a silver cigar case,
and jewelry and gloves to other members of the family, including a dozen pairs of kid gloves which he had custom-made
for a sister. To his mother he wrote, " I have been introduced into the very family of the King. Princes, Ministers
and Chamberlains have called upon me. My rank as consul
would never carry me into the position in which I now find
myself."

It was not long before ugly charges of financial irregulari-
ties in the American Consulate at Stuttgart began to drift
back to the United States. People who left money with Nast
to be transmitted to relatives in America complained that
the transfers were not made promptly, and in at least one

case, father Nast was asked to pay the money until his son could reimburse him. In 1863, the *Illinois Staatszeitung* of Chicago printed a report from its Stuttgart correspondent to the effect that the consul had charged exorbitant and illegal fees for his services, and the *Schwäbische Volkszeitung* demanded that he publish the rates that could be properly charged for visas, death certificates, and other consular services. William was also accused of gambling. A number of German-language papers in the United States reprinted the charges, and according to one account, William already was in prison. The elder Nast wrote frantically to his son for an explanation and indicated that he believed some of the attacks in the American press were really directed against him and the Methodist church. Mrs. Nast wrote from Stuttgart to reprimand her husband for not stopping the *Cincinnati Volksblatt* from publishing false charges against her son. In a pathetic letter Nast asked William to consider the effect of such accusations "among the enemies of the Cross" on the reputation of the church and prayed that a gracious Providence at least would defer the public disgrace of his son "until after General Conference and after my work (the *Commentary*) is before the public."

Consul Nast denied all the charges, attributed them to the publisher of one insignificant paper in Stuttgart, filed a libel suit against him, and authorized his father to prosecute German-American editors in the American courts. He insisted he was the victim of blackmailers and that he had never collected any fees not authorized by law and the regulations received from Washington. The elder Nast feared a Congressional investigation of the charges against his son and blamed all the latter's troubles on the vanity of this world which had made him live beyond his means. Actually, the episode was quickly forgotten, except by German creditors who continued to hound young Nast for years for the foolish debts he left behind in Germany. William returned to the United States in 1864. He was never charged, much less convicted, of malfeasance in office or corruption.

Equally disturbing to father Nast was the realization that only William, of all his children, was not safe in the Methodist fold. William apparently was little concerned about the status of his soul. Repeatedly, the father urged him to come to the Lord. In 1857, he was alarmed to learn that William was going to the theatre, which Nast regarded as the principal cause of the "moral enervation of our age" and "the most direct road to the grossest vices." Mrs. Nast shared her husband's concern about William's religion and prayed that William "might see his condition as a sinner and seek salvation."

Pleas and prayers were of no avail. William insisted that he believed in the Christian virtues, and he had more than the usual amount of compassion for his fellow men, but he could not accept Methodist theology. He wrote home less frequently as he grew older and tried to avoid the subject nearest his father's and mother's hearts. In 1887, he professed a love for people of all kinds and a readiness to forgive all his fellow-men, but he bluntly stated that he could not bear "saintly people" and had learned much about Christ from people who professed no religion. To such comments, father Nast always replied immediately with long theological discourses about salvation by grace through faith, and learned expositions of Methodist doctrine. While he was in England, William went to the London Music Hall to hear the evangelist, Sam Jones, and was thoroughly disgusted by his uncouth performance. He wrote his father that he hated all "shouting Methodists," and Nast could only reply that neither he nor his wife belonged in that category. As late as 1892, father and son were still debating theology. The parents continued to beg their son to accept the faith so that the family someday might be reunited in heaven, but they could do little more than offer daily prayers for William's soul. A year later, when William wrote that a little whiskey might improve his mother's health, the reply was a tirade against the use of liquor in any form or amount.

But the crowning blow had come when William announced he was going to marry a devout Roman Catholic and that the ceremony would be performed by a priest. The girl of his choice was Esther Benoist, a member of a respected family who lived in Oakland, nine miles from St. Louis, and who traced their ancestry back a century and a quarter to French fur traders in the Mississippi Valley. Father Nast, while on a tour of the Middle West, stopped off to visit his future daughter-in-law. He wrote his son Albert that she had lovely red hair, was passionately in love with William, and beautiful in "bearing . . . mind and heart." He was glad to be able to report that he found no crucifix in the Benoist home, "only a few beautiful portraits of the Virgin," and that the family had graciously asked the patriarch of Methodism to say grace at table. Nast also was pleased to note that two of Esther's sisters had married Protestants.

Nevertheless, when the Nasts were invited to the wedding, the leading German Methodist minister and editor was faced with a real crisis. If he went, Catholics would conclude that he had given his consent to the marriage, and to his son's promise that the children would become Catholics. If he stayed away, William would be deeply hurt. In letters to his son Albert, Nast discussed his mixed feelings. He wanted to go to the wedding, to please his son, but doubted whether his "official standing" in the Methodist church would make this possible. But if he refused to go, he would "raise up a partition wall" between himself and the young couple. Apparently, Mrs. Nast declined to go.

In the end, a father's love triumphed over the theological scruples of the Methodist. Nast wrote warmly to Esther and urged his children to write her also. He went to the wedding and stayed in St. Louis at the home of General C. B. Fisk, a member of the Methodist church. The priest who performed the ceremony apparently made every possible concession to Nast's Protestant scruples. He did not appear in sacerdotal robes, and according to Nast, "studiously seemed to avoid any ecclesiastical feature or blessing" and merely acted "under the authority of the state." Nast convinced himself that there was no vital difference between the Catholic and Protestant marriage ritual. He enjoyed the wedding party, was glad he came, and did not mind that the whole affair put him two hundred dollars in debt.

When the young couple's first child was born, William wrote his father that the boy would be baptized according to the mother's wishes. He professed unconcern about the forms of religion but added, significantly, that "being a boy, he will be influenced by reason when he grows up, and I can in a quiet way bring him under all the influences of our church." He asked his father to send the boy an inscribed copy of his *Commentary* as a birthday present. William's wife "will always remain a stranger to us," Nast wrote his son Albert on April 15, 1868, and expressed the fervent hope that William would remain a Protestant. When the daughter-in-law visited the Nasts, Mrs. Nast became gloomy and depressed, found it impossible to be "natural in her presence," and although Esther participated in the family devotions, her mother-in-law felt " unfit to deal with this power of darkness." As William's family multiplied, the elder Nasts were increasingly worried lest the girls become nuns and the boy a priest.

Meantime, William—" Mr. Disappoint," as his sister Fanny once called him—returned to the struggle to make money quickly. In 1865, he hoped to get a 20 per cent commission for selling railroad lands to European immigrants. Chief Justice Chase gave him a letter to Senator Pomeroy of Kansas, president of the Atchinson and Pikes Peak Railroad, and the latter in turn introduced William to James Wadsworth, a railroad director from New York. William wrote his father that he had been " closeted with millionaires in New York and Philadelphia," and outlined a grand plan to import hundreds of laborers and colonizers from Europe. In 1870, William was speculating in Florida real estate. The next year he asked his father for an introduction to Jay Cooke, the Philadelphia banking magnate who had entertained Nast at his home on Gibraltar Island, in Lake Erie. In 1875, William was operating as a stockbroker on Wall Street and living happily with his family in New York in quarters that looked out upon the palisades of the Hudson. But Charles Nordhoff wrote the elder Nast that William was " like Archimedes, who had a lever powerful enough to move the world—but could not get a fulcrum," and urged that the young man get out of New York, make a new start in the West, and get over the " dreamy belief " that one could acquire a fortune without working for it.

Presently, William left his family to seek greener pastures abroad, and before long his wife was so hard pressed for funds that on several occasions her father-in-law sent her small amounts of money. Her husband's absence extended into years, for fortune always was for William just around the corner. William sent packages to his children but seldom wrote his wife. In one of his infrequent letters, he wrote from London, on July 22, 1876, that he had invented and was building a machine to dry and bale straw, which he would sell to paper-mill owners at a profit of $5,000 a week. The first machine, built at a cost of $2,500, turned out to be a complete failure, and the next year, William's wife was selling her property in Missouri to meet taxes. William meantime had gone to Paris to organize a stock company to manufacture paper from baled straw and manure. He had figured out exactly how much manure the horses of London would produce, and how he could sell it to farmers for fertilizer and for the manufacture of paper. He was sure that his new process would revolutionize newspaper publishing, and he sent his father a sample of the paper, and forecast an annual profit of $200,000.

While William remained abroad, his wife's holdings were being dissipated to meet the daily expenses of the family. When William wrote home, his letters were full of affection, but he vowed he would not return to eat his wife's bread, except as a "victor" in his struggle for fame and fortune. He wrote occasionally to his mother and less often to his father, who continued to beg him to come home and offered to send him the necessary passage money. Albert thought his older brother had deserted his family and would never return.

In 1890, William finally came home and had a successful reunion with his devoted wife at the home of a relative in Evanston, Illinois. A Chicago paper reported the incident under the headline "Separated for Thirteen Years, Mr. and

Mrs. William Nast Become Reconciled and Resume Marital Relations" and added that at one time, the wife's personal fortune had amounted to $300,000. In a long letter to his father, dated September 29, 1890, William reviewed his trials and failures—"from being a Consul as a mere boy, then ten years . . . in that great whirlpool the Stock Exchange of New York where there is no respect or veneration of persons," and men "stand nearly naked before the Stock Exchange high priest, the Stock Broker; and then for fifteen years a complete change of life in a new field with new men . . . struggling, pushing, persevering against impossible odds." The letter listed all his failures without attributing a single one to his own shortcomings. With this letter we may leave the story of this generous, essentially kind, restless and utterly impractical man, who was the major problem of the Nast family. He died in 1893 and was buried in Calvary Cemetery in St. Louis. His son Condé, educated at Georgetown University, became the publisher of *Vogue, Vanity Fair* and several other periodicals.

The relationship between Nast and his second son, Albert, was in sharp contrast with that with William. Albert was much like his father, a devout Methodist, an ordained minister and a scholar, with an innate shyness that made him far happier at the editorial desk than in the pulpit. The voluminous correspondence between father and son began when Albert was just a boy and continued throughout their lifetime. In it, the elder Nast unburdened himself on everything from his occasional difficulties and misunderstandings with "Ma" and his periods of depression, to matters of finance, theology and the church.

When Albert was eleven years old, Nast decided to send him to a school in Kornthal, Württemberg, so that the boy would get a thorough German education in a proper religious environment. The lad remained in the cold, rigid atmosphere of this German school, far from home and without complaint, from 1857 to 1861, but when the headmaster advised that he remain for another two years to complete his training, he became so homesick that the parents decided it would be best for Mrs. Nast and her daughters to go to Germany to be near her son. Nast asked the Lord for guidance, and Mrs. Nast's physician recommended a change of climate to improve her health. Nast accompanied the family to New York, and seized the opportunity to preach in several churches while in the East, to attend the New York Conference, and to visit with Charles Nordhoff, "his former foster-son." He went on to Boston, where he renewed his friendship with Harriet Beecher Stowe's husband, whom he had met in Cincinnati and who was living in Andover and who introduced him to the editor of the *Bibliotheca Sacra*. In Boston, Nast also called on the lieutenant-governor of Massachusetts and then went to New Haven to visit one of the professors at Yale.[1]

We may be sure that Albert, now fifteen, was delighted to see his mother and sisters after four years in a foreign land, for the boy's letters to his father reveal that he found neither the students nor the headmaster at Kornthal particularly congenial. He fell in love with a girl, and wrote nostalgically about another girl he had known in America, and his adolescent emotions temporarily affected his grades, although he spent thirty-seven hours a week in the classroom, and twenty-three in study. He learned German thoroughly, and corresponded regularly with his father about his religious progress. In letters admonishing him to keep at his books, the father pointed out that ten hours a day devoted to study were not excessive, and that he himself frequently worked twelve to fourteen hours. Albert's marks were not always the best; he had difficulty with Latin and arithmetic, and sometimes became discouraged. While in Germany, he was "confirmed" in the Lutheran church, with his father's consent, but with the understanding that this rite did not involve a pledge to remain a Lutheran forever. The mother advised her son to be diligent in daily prayer and Bible reading, to be punctual, to exercise careful economy, and to observe the Sabbath. Albert received a thorough elementary education, and in 1861, he was able to write his father a long letter in French. But in 1864, when he was back in the United States, attending school in Lima, New York, he finally unburdened himself to his father in a letter in which he said, "I had four years . . . in Kornthal, which I can with a slight pricking of my conscience compare to a civilized convent or a delightful prison."

Mrs. Nast's letters to her husband from Germany show that she was never happy in that country, although she had her children with her. She found living costs high and continued to ask her hard-pressed husband for money. She did not get on well with her in-laws in Württemberg, and she referred to the German people as a stupid "pack of fools," although she quickly added that her husband was an exception and was German only because he used the language. She was enraged by the pro-Confederate sentiments she found in some German business circles and in the press. Nast's relatives tried to tell her how to manage her affairs, and after several rather sharp exchanges with her husband on the matter, both decided to drop the subject from their future correspondence. When Nast's aunt made disparaging remarks about the *Commentary* and suggested that there were more learned theologians in Germany than her nephew, Mrs. Nast was furious. She complained about the poor quality of soap in Germany and sighed for "Proctor and Gamble's Rosin Soap"; she found the German Christmas gloomy and too solemn; she hated the drinking and singing that went on on Sundays, although she learned to drink a quart of beer daily for medicinal purposes because she decided tea and water upset her intestinal tract. She distrusted some of the German Methodist missionaries who came over from the United States, reported that the Lutherans were especially hostile to Methodism, and accused her husband's friend, Jacoby, of diverting missionary funds into his own pocket and poking "his nose into everybody's business, Jew-like." Among the missionaries, only Brother Nippert, in her judgment, was "a true American."

To offset these unpleasant experiences, Mrs. Nast had her son William, who "gets handsomer every day," and her daughter "Josie," whose beauty elicited comment in Stuttgart circles. She enjoyed attending court and other festivities, to which she gained admission through her son, the consul, and she was proud of a Fourth of July celebration in Stuttgart which he had arranged. Albert came from Kornthal each week end to visit the family, who lived in a four-room third-floor apartment, which Mrs. Nast had rented. But the mother sometimes had her doubts about Albert. She thought he was homely and shy, not too bright and a slow thinker, and perhaps should go to West Point, where he would be "supported by the government."

Much in Mrs. Nast's letters must have been very depressing to her husband, but they also reveal that "Ma" was genuinely homesick for "Pa," as he was still more for her. Mrs. Nast vacillated between coming home and staying longer in Stuttgart to guard her son William from his "gay friends," but in July, 1864, she decided to bring the family back to the United States. She expressed a desire to visit Niagara Falls and Chicago, en route home, and she made it abundantly clear that she did not want to live in Cincinnati, where she thought the climate so bad that it would kill her in two years. Before departing for the United States, she informed her husband that "William will draw on you for $500 to get us home."

After seven years in a German school, Albert was enrolled in Genesee College and Wesleyan Seminary in Lima, in Livingston County, New York. His sister Fanny went with him, and they lived at the home of Professor S. A. Lattimore, A. M. The cost to the family was a little over $400 a year for the two children. Because Albert had become greatly interested in music by this time, his father had a piano sent to the Lattimore home so that the boy could do his practising. In Lima, Albert combined studying with such pleasant diversions as sleighing parties to Avon, candy-pulling socials, music, collecting stamps, joining a Greek-letter society, and membership in the Genesee Lyceum. He kept a diary in which he diligently recorded the progress of his studies, "the blessed time at prayer meeting" when "souls were flocking to the mercy seat," and comments on current political issues. His sister Josephine, on a visit in Brooklyn, chided her father for sending such a promising boy to such "a one horse college" populated with "blockheads," and before long Albert himself hoped for an opportunity to go to a better school.

Whatever may have been the defects of faculty and curriculum at Lima, there was no lack of religious fervor. Professor Lattimore wrote Nast about frequent revivals among the students and of Albert's interest in class and prayer meetings, where he was "quickened in his religious zeal." Albert wrote that God had saved his soul and forgiven his sins and that his studies were now improving. Albert apparently experienced all the emotional upheavals of a conversion, testified in open meeting, and happily reported that his sister, too, was "rejoicing and glorifying God." Both joined the church, and Albert commented, "I would be glad to die for I know I would be received in heaven."

After leaving Lima, Albert worked for a time for the New York *Methodist*, where he began to reveal his talents for editorial work. He managed his personal affairs so well that shortly after his arrival in New York, he was able to send home ten dollars, four for "Pa," four for "Ma," and one each for his two sisters. In 1866, he decided to enter the ministry and hoped for an opportunity to attend Wesleyan, in Middletown, Connecticut. Samuel F. Odell, a friend of Nast and a member of the board of managers of the Methodist Missionary Society, offered to help the lad, nominated him for the scholarship which he had established at the college, and agreed to meet Albert's expenses for board, fuel and laundry. William sent his brother some clothes, and thus fitted out, Albert was able to continue his education. College expenses were so low that when Albert graduated, a silk hat and a broadcloth suit cost him more than the normal fees for a school year.

Albert profited greatly from his years at Wesleyan. He was a good student, without being a brilliant one: he read widely, was fascinated by geology, and learned to love the works of Schiller. He heard Charles Dickens lecture at the college, enjoyed much good music, went on student excursions, and danced and drank at college parties. His father admonished him to be more economical and warned against flirtations with the girls as unbecoming to a young man destined for the ministry. During vacations spent with the

Odells in New York, Albert heard Henry Ward Beecher preach and attended a concert by Ole Bull, the famous Norwegian violinist.

At twenty-one, he was still struggling over the choice of a vocation. He told his mother he had grave doubts whether he would succeed as a preacher, but in preparation, he gave up smoking and card playing, attended religious exercises, and prayed fervently for "a full blessing." In 1868, the *Christliche Apologete* proudly reported Albert's graduation, with an A. B. degree from Wesleyan, and referred to the two senior essays which he had written, one on classical education and the other on "Popular Amusements." Albert won the prize in English composition, and the proud father pointed out that the essays were "marked by originality, freshness, and courageous thinking," and a "classical style." [2]

Albert already had given music lessons in Berea, and his father hoped that the time would come when he might join the faculty of Wallace College, and continue his father's "great work" in the ministry and the field of education. While a senior at Wesleyan, Albert had delivered his first sermon. He reported that he felt "no inspiration from above" and would await a "baptism of fire" before he would venture into the pulpit again. Despite his own misgivings, he received an exhorter's license in January 1869 and before the end of the year was regularly ordained, without further formal theological training, and began preaching in German to German Methodist congregations. His nearsightedness forced him to use glasses to read his notes. He liked the Germans and knew their language, but he felt he lacked "the tie of nationality" necessary to succeed in the German Methodist church. In due course, he held pastorates in Cincinnati, Pittsburgh, Columbus, Cleveland, Pomeroy and Malta, Ohio, but he became more and more convinced that he really belonged in academic or editorial work. He disliked the more boisterous manifestations of Methodist meetings and thought "calm and patient instruction" more valuable than noisy revivals. He sent outlines of his sermons to his father and sought his advice, but the elder Nast finally had to accept the inevitable and make plans to get his son into the editorial office of the *Apologete,* or on the faculty of Wallace College.

Mrs. Nast, who thought her son was too much of a scholarly recluse, urged him to meet more Americans and to set aside an evening or two a week for congenial friends. When Albert married Sarah McDermott, in 1876, there was further discussion of whether he should stay in the German ministry, but his father could reassure him from his own experience that an English-speaking wife was not a handicap. Brother William had advised Albert to marry only a woman of means.

Albert struggled along for some years in the career of minister, for which he knew he was not really fitted. He complained about the pitifully low salaries, which were often in arrears. In 1877, from Columbus, he wrote his father, " I am but a poor preacher at best" and expressed his desire for a teaching post where he could combine the secular with the religious. When he was finally transferred to a congregation thirty miles from a railroad and had to live in a badly run-down parsonage, the elder Nast was outraged that his son should be sent to such " a fourth class pastorate." The church at Malta marked the nadir of Albert's preaching career.

In 1875, Albert was considered for a professorship at a German college affiliated with Iowa Wesleyan but did not get the appointment. Two years later, he declined a post at a moribund Methodist women's college in Cincinnati. In

1880, he joined the faculty of Illinois Wesleyan, in Bloomington, as a teacher of Latin and German, but resigned in 1883,
without another position in sight. His teaching experience
had been successful, and he had made plans to build a home
in Bloomington, but his wife became ill with tuberculosis,
and died in 1883, leaving two small children. Nast tried
unsuccessfully to get his son another faculty appointment, at
Syracuse, Allegheny, Boston University, DePauw, Kenyon,
and "the new Adelbert University in Cleveland," now
Western Reserve University. In 1884, Albert Nast became
assistant editor of the *Apologete* and eight years later succeeded his father as editor-in-chief, a post which he filled with
distinction until 1918, when he resigned, the innocent victim
of the anti-German hysteria of World War I to which the
Methodists, including some German Methodists, had surrendered as uncritically as many other Americans. In 1892,
Albert received an honorary Doctor of Divinity degree from
Ohio University, and ten years later, he was similarly honored
by Wesleyan, his alma mater.

Josephine, the Nasts' attractive elder daughter, attended
school with her brother Albert in Kornthal and in Lima, but
was never impressed with Genesee College. After a visit
with friends in Brooklyn, she commented "there is quite a
difference between a Yale student and an Asbury or Genesee
student." "Josie" was a vivacious young lady, interested in
the theatre, nice clothes, and sprightly company. She had
none of her father's somber outlook on life and thought her
mother did not give her enough freedom. Whenever she was
in New York, with the Nordhoffs, she went to Coney Island
and the menageries and was so delighted with the big city that
she considered finding employment there as a governess.

In 1861, Michael J. Cramer wrote to Albert Nast that

he was engaged to his sister, Josephine, and the elder Nast did all he could to promote the match. He believed Cramer was a devout Methodist and the latter always referred to Nast as his " spiritual father " and the Race Street Church in Cincinnati as his "spiritual birthplace." Josephine, despite her father's admonitions to give her suitor more encouragement, remained unimpressed by Cramer's "soft, sickening love letters," so full of self-praise. If there ever had been an understanding between Cramer and "Josie," it was broken off in 1863, and shortly thereafter Cramer announced his engagement to the youngest sister of Ulysses S. Grant. Nast officiated at their marriage. During the Civil War, Cramer worked in military hospitals as an army chaplain and claimed to have converted many dying soldiers to Methodism. When Grant became President, he gave political jobs to his relatives, and his brother-in-law became minister to Copenhagen and later to Switzerland. In 1888, having somehow acquired a doctor of sacred theology degree in the meantime, Cramer became a professor at Boston University, and in 1897, published a book entitled *Ulysses S. Grant, Conversations and Unpublished Letters.*

In February 1867, " Josie " informed her father that she had given her heart to Dr. William Joseph Andrews, a young homeopath, and the marriage took place on April 25, 1867. The young couple had little with which to begin housekeeping in Muncie, Indiana, and before long, the bride was selling her few jewels to buy surgical instruments and medical books for her husband. Josephine did not like Muncie, with its "hog and hominy diet," primitive living conditions and patients who were slow in paying their doctor's bills. Her father worried about the doctor because he was not "a renewed man," and wondered whether his daughter had chosen wisely. The economic and other troubles of the Andrews continued even after they moved to Newark, New Jersey. The doctor became an alcoholic and had to go to a sanatorium before he was finally cured of his affliction. Nast continued to worry about their finances, and feared his daughter did not have sufficient religion to cope with her family problems. Josie admitted that she did not feel at home among either professing Christians or the worldly, and the correspondence between father and daughter revealed a growing incompatibility but no lack of affection. The marriage of Josephine and the doctor, an essentially warm-hearted and charming person, endured despite hardships and was blessed with three children, one of whom died in early infancy.

Franzeska Wilhelmina (Fanny) Nast, the youngest of the Nast children, was born in 1848 and died in 1913. A spirited girl, she loved pretty things and did not fit too easily into the German Methodist pattern, though she always was a loyal church member. At thirteen, she stopped attending a German Sunday school and went to an English church. She was not happy in the girl's department of the school in Lima, New York, and her parents were advised to take her home. She transferred to Berea, where she got along quite well, but found life in the village rather dull. In 1866, she graduated—the first woman graduate of Wallace College. As with his other children, Nast was concerned lest Fanny was slipping in religious matters and too much interested in clothes and too little in prayer meetings.

In 1871, Fanny was courted by William A. Gamble, a shy, quiet young man, whose family was associated with the Proctor and Gamble Company of Cincinnati. William was the son of James Gamble, an Irish immigrant soap maker who was converted to Methodism, became a warm friend of

Nast, and invited the latter to preach at his home during his early missionary activities in Cincinnati. The elder Gamble was one of the founders of the Proctor and Gamble Company, which in its early days employed many German Methodists. William Gamble received a considerable fortune from his father, and after his marriage to Fanny, the Nast family benefitted materially from holdings of Proctor and Gamble stock. Fanny Nast and William Gamble were married in Berea, on October 3, 1872, and before many years, the elder Nasts were relieved of most of their financial worries. They spent many years in the Gamble home in Cincinnati, or at Lakeside during the summer months, where the Gambles owned a number of lots and three cottages.

Fanny's devotion to her family, and especially to her father, was one of the old man's greatest satisfactions in his declining years. She showered her parents with gifts on special days, and saw to it that they were never in want. She had no children and her husband died in 1897; so she channeled many of her activities into Methodist church work in Cincinnati. She sponsored lectures and Bible readings, and engaged in a round of social activities centering largely in the church. She was especially interested in foreign missions, to which she contributed lavishly throughout her life. She endowed a professorship at Berea in honor of her father and made generous gifts to many Methodist charitable institutions, including Christ Hospital in Cincinnati and the Elizabeth Gamble Deaconess Home. She also contributed to the Salvation Army and many philanthropies, and the residue of her fortune was willed to the Methodist church for the benefit of retired "worn-out preachers."

14

THE CLOSING YEARS

William Nast's life span far exceeded the Biblical three score and ten, and he lived long enough to reap the satisfaction and rewards of a distinguished career as editor, author, theologian and messenger of the cross. He was universally recognized and revered as the pioneer saint of German Methodism. Parents gave his name to their children, and he was godfather to the offspring of a number of his fellow ministers. An inveterate traveller, he filled pulpits in many parts of the country, from New Orleans to Canada, and Omaha to the Atlantic seaboard. People flocked to hear him preach, whether he spoke in English or in German, and were always impressed by his sincere piety and humility. He was in constant demand to dedicate new churches and enjoyed every opportunity to get around the country to see his fellow German Methodists.

As early as 1866, when *Harper's Weekly* printed the portraits of "Distinguished Men of Methodism," to mark the centenary of American Methodism, Nast's picture was among them, and he was described as an eminent scholar, writer and pulpit orator.[1] McKendree College made him an honorary Doctor of Divinity. He was the first Methodist and the first German minister to be the guest of Jay Cooke on Gibraltar Island,[2] who entertained many of the nation's most prominent citizens at his Lake Erie mansion. The husband of the author of *Uncle Tom's Cabin* was his good friend. Nast was a delegate to many meetings, and an important member of many committees of the Methodist church. In 1884, the year observed as the fiftieth anniversary of German Methodism in the United States, he preached jubilee sermons in a number of cities. A Nast Memorial Church was built in Springfield, Illinois, and dedicated by Albert Nast in 1891, because his father thought his health was too precarious to permit him to attend. In the same year, however, he was a delegate to the Ecumenical Methodist Conference and was received at the White House by President Harrison. In 1887, Nast preached at the quarterly meeting of the Methodist Conference in Chicago and rode in the phaeton of the chief of police to a picnic dinner in Hyde Park. The next year, he was the guest of the president of Drew Theological Seminary in Madison, New Jersey, and visited Dickinson College in Pennsylvania on his return journey to Ohio.

Nast was one of the founders of the Berea orphanage as well as Wallace College, where his name is remembered through a Nast professorship of theology and a building known as Nast Theological Seminary. In 1902 the academy German Methodists started in 1888 in Chinkiang, China, was renamed William Nast College. Three years earlier, the students had sent a beautiful black lacquer table as a gift to the patriarch of German Methodism on which likenesses of Methodist bishops were inlaid with mother-of-pearl. The principal was Carl F. Kupfer, a Wallace College graduate.

In June 1892 when Nast celebrated his eighty-fifth birthday at the Gamble home in Avondale, the men's chorus of the German city mission serenaded the venerable pioneer of Methodism by candlelight on the lawn and presented him with a bouquet of flowers; and Nippert, Golder, and other German Methodist veterans came to pay their respects. The porch of the Gamble home was strung with Japanese lanterns, there were a few speeches, and the men's chorus ended the program with "God be with you till we meet again." The *Cincinnati Volksblatt* joined in this tribute to a distinguished Cincinnatian. In 1895, the *Apologete* offered an etching of Nast, done in Chicago, as a prize to new subscribers, and on the occasion of Nast's eighty-eighth birthday, the *Cincinnati Volksblatt* printed a congratulatory article. On his ninetieth birthday, English and German Methodists again made a pilgrimage to the home in Avondale, and the local press carried accounts of his long career. The *Apologete* reprinted a sermon delivered in Cincinnati fifty years before, telegrams came from many cities and from abroad, and several English Methodist journals took notice of the occasion. Mrs. Nast presented her husband with her picture to comfort him when she should be gone and until they could be reunited in heaven.[3]

In later years, the financial status of the Nast family improved considerably, primarily because of good advice from William Gamble and generous help from their daughter Fanny. The Gambles saw to it that the old couple were comfortable. At one time, Nast's salary as editor of the

Apologete was $2500 a year, but there is no way to calculate accurately his income from other sources. A receipt from the Internal Revenue Office, for 1872, preserved among the Nast papers, shows that he paid a tax of $33.30 on $1332, the amount of taxable income beyond a $5,000 exemption. Tax receipts from Cuyahoga County for 1870 and 1872 show that Nast owned a lot in the village of Brooklyn valued at $978 and property in Berea listed at $1165.

In 1882, William Gamble bought railroad stock for his father-in-law which yielded 8 per cent, but Nast also had stock in the Hamilton and Dayton Railroad which yielded nothing. He was an easy target for stock salesmen. When his will was probated in Hamilton County, it showed holdings in several railroads, a steel company, a cattle company, and two hundred shares in an Idaho gold mine, valued at $2.50 a share. Nast also had some Cincinnati bank stock, bonds of the Lakeside Company, two bonds of the Freedman's Aid and Southern Education Society, valued at $500 each; but his best investment was twenty-two shares of Proctor and Gamble, valued at the time at $395 a share. When the estate was finally closed in 1901, by Albert Nast, who acted as executor and administrator, the assets amounted to just under $25,000. Among the various expenses paid by the executor was $25 to the bishop who conducted Nast's funeral services.

Rich with honors, and fairly well endowed with worldly goods in their later years, the Nasts nevertheless were not spared the ravages of advancing age. Both had several prolonged periods of illness. Nast suffered periodically from sick headaches and in 1877 asked a nephew in Germany to send him *Magentropfen*, which he believed were an efficacious remedy for his chronic affliction. On another occasion, he ordered a "box Medicine high Potences" from St. Louis. A double hernia proved especially troublesome in his later years, and homeopathic remedies were ineffective for his chronic hay fever and asthma. In 1887, he spent some time in the Cleveland Homeopathic Hospital; on another occasion he was at Clifton Springs in New York for treatments; and in 1894 he went to Chicago to consult two specialists for what he thought was a mysterious abdominal tumor but was so quickly restored that he was able to preach in several Chicago churches. He tried the best wines for medicinal purposes but found them no more effective than the cheaper grades.

Mrs. Nast's health always weighed heavily on her husband's mind. She apparently had great faith in patent medicines and kept a well-stocked medicine chest, which included, among other things, Winchester Hypophosphates of Lime and Soda. In 1890, Nast wrote Albert that his mother was in poor health, and that the doctor thought her trouble was more mental than physical. The physician added, " I confess that such cases . . . make me sometimes sceptical about religious experience." Nast could only try " to point " his wife " to the Saviour." He urged her to be more patient about her trials, but she was frequently discouraged because her prayers seemed to remain unanswered. In 1890, Mrs. Nast had a heart attack; two years later she was in a hospital in Mt. Clemens, Michigan. In 1896, Nast wrote to Albert, " Ma is an enigma to me."

More serious than these physical afflictions, from Nast's point of view, were the depressions from which he suffered periodically. There is no adequate data to explain them. As early as 1862, Mrs. Nast observed that her husband would always be discontented and uneasy, because he had " an uneasy mind," and Nast admitted that he yielded " too much to gloomy forebodings [and] despondencies " and hoped his children would not inherit this affliction from him. His children urged him to see and talk to more people, and Josephine wrote in 1877, "Please don't save yourself for the holiness people, for if they are so happy, they have no need of you."

As he grew older, Nast frequently worried about his own salvation. "The cause of my low spirits is that dreadful power of unbelief," he wrote Albert as early as 1868. "How strange that I can preach the word of faith with power and yet do not appreciate it myself! that I should feed others with manna and hunger myself!" Albert told him to be less introspective, pointed out that joyousness should be "an integral part of piety," and advised him to read Cicero's *De Senectute* and take it to heart.

The correspondence between father and son contains many references to "inner conflicts." Nast longed for the day when he might be entirely free of his "melancholy attacks." In 1888, he wrote a fellow Methodist, "I have been crucified with Him, but I have not yet realized the power of his resurrection life." Sometimes he found relief in prayer, on other occasions he found it ineffective. Sometimes he thought he was losing his mind and ought to go to a sanitarium. Fortunately, these spells of despondency usually did not last long, and he would be able to tell his son that "the storm is over." Shortly before her death, Mrs. Nast suggested to her daughter that she sing hymns to her father to rouse him from his depression, and in one of her last letters, written from Lakeside on March 14, 1898, she observed, "He thinks he is a great sinner," so sing him a hymn which says he is one, and "you know he must always take the opposite stand."

Eliza McDowell Nast died shortly thereafter, thus ending a marriage of sixty-two years. She is said to have died while reciting the Twenty-third Psalm. William Nast died on May

16, 1899, probably from pneumonia. The *Apologete*, which had featured so many descriptions of Methodist deathbed scenes, described the last hours of its former editor in great detail. According to the account, Nast died with a prayer on his lips and a number of "last words" (among which were "Come Lord Jesus"), which were recorded and were long cherished by the faithful. The Methodist deaconesses sang "Saved by Grace" and "Wonderful Words of Life," and their singing was frequently interrupted by "Amens" and "Halleluliahs" from the dying patriarch, whose countenance was illumined by the glory of God.[4] Nast was buried from Trinity Methodist Church in Cincinnati, which was crowded by church dignitaries from various conferences and hundreds of plain people who came to pay their last respects to a great figure in the life of their church. A bishop delivered the funeral oration; telegrams and letters arrived from many places, and memorial services were held in a number of cities.

The *Northwestern Christian Advocate* for May 24, 1899, carried a long obituary, and a week later printed a poem, "In Memoriam," by President Warren of Boston University, dedicated to "Swabia's son," containing the stanza,

> Thy name and fame
> Two peoples claim . . .
> Two worlds can see
> Thy legacy. . . .

Nast and his wife lie buried in Spring Grove Cemetery in Cincinnati, where, in 1923, a group of Methodists assembled for ceremonies which marked the sixtieth anniversary of the founding of the Central German Methodist Conference. Many must have stopped to read again the inscription on the monument which marks the last resting place of the pioneer of

German Methodism. The inscription notes Nast's sincere piety, his gentleness and unfeigned humility, his long and varied services to the Methodist cause, and the virtues of his wife and helpmate of over sixty years. Chiselled in stone beneath these is a passage from Timothy, which this gentle, kind and forgiving soul, so concerned with the innate depravity of man and the need for salvation, probably would have approved. It reads, "This is a faithful saying, and worthy of all acceptation, that Christ Jesus came into the world to save sinners, of whom I am chief."

NOTES

1

[1] *Allgemeine Deutsche Biographie* (Leipzig, 1886), XXIII, 270-71.

[2] See "Dr. Wm. Nast's Religious Experience Told by Himself," in *Northwestern Christian Advocate* (Chicago), May 31, 1899, pp. 6-7; an account by Nast's son, Albert, in *Der Christliche Apologete* (Cincinnati), May 25, 1899 (hereafter cited as *C. A.*); and Adam Miller, *Experience of German Methodist Preachers* (Cincinnati, 1859), pp. 136-143, and *Origin and Progress of the German Missions in the Methodist Episcopal Church* (Cincinnati, 1843).

[3] Mörike's charming fairy tale, "Das Stuttgarter Hutzelmänn-lein," is located largely in Blaubeuren. See *Gesammelte Erzählungen* (Leipzig, 1897), pp. 112-252.

[4] Gutzkow referred to the book as "the yeast of Germany's intellectual ferment." See Karl Gutzkow, *Rückblicke auf mein Leben* (Berlin, 1875), pp. 140, 290-91.

[5] *C. A.*, April 25, 1861. See also *Allgemeine Deutsche Bi-ographie* (Leipzig, 1875), II, 172-79; *Encyclopedia of the Social Sciences* (New York, 1930), II, 481-82. For Strauss, see *Encyclopedia of the Social Sciences* (New York, 1934), XIV, 416-17; *Allgemeine Deutsche Biographie*

(Leipzig, 1893), XXXVI, 538-48; C. A., February 11, 1897, June 15, 1899; and Nast's "Recollections of David Friedrich Strauss," in *The New Princeton Review*, IV (1887), 343-48. For this article, Nast received $30. Strauss' work was also a major factor in the progression of such American theologians as Theodore Parker from a relatively orthodox Unitarianism to their later views about the nature of Jesus.

2

[1] See William Henry Egle, *Notes and Queries*, Second Series (Philadelphia, 1895), pp. 192-97; Sherman Day, *Historical Collections of Pennsylvania* (Philadelphia, 1843), pp. 289-90; and Luther R. Kelker, *History of Dauphin County, Pennsylvania* (New York, 1907), I, 429-435.

[2] C. A., February 23, 1880.

[3] I am indebted to Professor Landon Warner and Registrar S. R. McGowan of Kenyon College for these details.

3

[1] See W. J. Warner, *The Wesleyan Movement in the Industrial Revolution* (London, 1930).

[2] John Wesley prepared a book entitled *Primitive Physic* (London, 1747), which is a strange mixture of good and bad suggestions for the health and cure of the body.

[3] See, e. g., *The Doctrine and Discipline of the Methodist Episcopal Church* (New York, 1808).

[4] See Sydney G. Dimond, *The Psychology of the Methodist Revival* (London, 1926), especially the first four chapters.

[5] C. A., October 20, 1879. For a discussion in psychological terms, see Dimond, *op. cit.*, Chapter VII.

[6] See Charles A. Johnson, *The Frontier Camp Meeting* (Dallas, 1953).

[7] Charles T. Greve, *Centennial History of Cincinnati* (3 vols., Chicago, 1904), I, 362,524.

[8] See Wade Crawford Barclay, *Early American Methodism, 1769-1844* (2 vols., New York, 1949); William Warren Sweet, *Religion on the American Frontier, 1783-1840* (Chicago, 1946), IV, *The Methodists*; J. M. Buckley, *A History of Methodists in the United States* (New York,

1896); W. W. Sweet, *The Rise of Methodism in the West* (Cincinnati, 1920); Samuel W. Williams, *Pictures of Early Methodism in Ohio* (Cincinnati, 1909); Elizabeth K. Nottingham, *Methodism and the Frontier: Indiana Proving Ground* (New York, 1941); and Francis I. Moats, " The Rise of Methodism in the Middle West," in *The Mississippi Valley Historical Review*, XV (1928-29), 69-88.

4

[1] See *C. A.*, January 11, 1839, February 22, 1894, January 24, 1895, May 25, 1899; *Northwestern Christian Advocate* (Chicago), May 31, 1899, pp. 6-7; *Souvenir of the Ninetieth Anniversary of the Organization of German Methodism at William Nast Memorial Church* (Cincinnati, 1928) for an account by Nast's son Albert; and Adam Miller, *Origin and Progress of the German Missions of the Methodist Episcopal Church* (Cincinnati, 1843), pp. 136-143.

[2] A. C. Morehouse, *Incidents of the Early History of Methodism in England and America* (New York, n. d.), p. 30. See, also, Ludwig S. Jacoby, *Geschichte des Britischen Methodismus* (Bremen, 1870), pp. 186-338, which deal with German Methodism.

[3] See Henry A. and Kate B. Ford, *History of Cincinnati, Ohio* (Cleveland, 1881), especially pp. 127-146, and Charles Cist, *Cincinnati in 1841* (Cincinnati, 1841).

[4] Quoted in Adam Miller, *Origin and Progress of the German Missions in the Methodist Episcopal Church* (Cincinnati, 1843), pp. 26-27.

[5] *Ibid.*, pp. 28-30.

[6] *The Methodist Quarterly Review*, LXIII (1881), 13-14.

[7] For further comments on Nast's activities, see James B. Finley, *Sketches of Western Methodism* (Cincinnati, 1855), p. 117.

[8] *C. A.*, November 29, 1844; also Heinrich Mann, *Ludwig S. Jacoby* (Bremen, 1892) and Ludwig S. Jacoby, *Handbuch des Methodismus* (Bremen, 1855).

[9] The biography was published in Cincinnati in 1889 and sold for a dollar.

[10] See W. G. Bek, " The Community at Bethel, Missouri and Its Offspring at Aurora, Oregon," in *German-American Annals*, New Series, VII, 257-76, 306-28; VIII, 15-44, 76-81; and " A German Communistic Society in Missouri " in *Missouri Historical Review*, III, 5-74, 99-125.

5

[1] *C. A.*, February 8, 1858.

[2] See *Geschichte der Zentral Deutschen Konferenz*, edited by C. Golder, John H. Horst, J. G. Schaal (Cincinnati, n. d.).

[3] *C. A.*, March 6, 1890.

[4] *Ibid.*, November 21, 1881.

[5] After serving the church for many years, Miller became a practicing physician in Chicago. *C. A.*, for June 30, 1879 advertised that Brother Miller, M.D., was doing a book on " Plain Talks to the Sick: with Directions for Homeopathic Treatment," which would sell for a dollar.

[6] *C. A.*, June 21, 1894.

[7] For a list of German Methodist ministers, see Golder, Horst and Schall, *op. cit.* In each case, the time of conversion and membership is indicated and generally with such phrases as " led to the Lord," " converted to God," " mightily renewed, "learned to know his Lord," " found salvation from sin," " found peace in Christ," " was born again."

[8] The itinerary of the circuit riders was regularly reported in the *C. A.*

[9] *C. A.*, October 5, 1899.

[10] *Ibid.*, January 10, 1881.

[11] *Ibid.*, August 16, 1846.

[12] *Ibid.*, April 16, 1895.

[13] *Ibid.*, July 7, 1859.

[14] The *Christian Advocate*, CIX (September 19, 1935), 845.

[15] See *C. A.*, October 7, 1867; May 31, 1869.

[16] August N. Wexelberg, who joined the church in 1842, maintained a " mission wagon " for many years, on which he had painted " Mission Wagon. Papers and Tracts in American, Bohemian, Danish, French and German. Free. Orders taken for Bibles and Testaments in about every language."—*C. A.*, July 21, 1892.

[17] *C. A.*, January 7, 1858.

[18] *Ibid.*, May 25, 1863.

[19] *Ibid.*, September 10, 1891.

[20] For early churches in Ohio, see John M. Barker, *History of Ohio Methodism* (Cincinnati, 1898) and Wallace G. Smeltzer, *Methodism on the Headwaters of the Ohio* (Nashville, 1951). For the spread of German Methodist missions, see, e. g., *Thirty-first Annual Report of the Missionary Society of the Methodist Episcopal Church* (New York, 1850),

pp. 33-64; *Forty-Fifth Annual Report* (New York, 1864), pp. 93-95; and *Fifty-Second Annual Report* (New York, 1871), pp. 121-122.

[21] *C. A.*, May 19, 1853.

[22] *Ibid.*, June 30, 1859.

[23] *Ibid.*, January 6, 1868.

[24] *Ibid.*, March 2, April 20, 1874.

[25] See also Adam J. Loeppert, "The Harvest of an Immigrant Scholar," in the *Christian Advocate*, CIX (September 19, 1935).

6

[1] *C. A.*, August 19, 1858.

[2] *Ibid.*, January 12, 1854.

[3] *Ibid.*, August 29, 1845, August 19, 1858, February 14, 1889.

[4] *Ibid.*, January 29, 1891.

[5] *Ibid.*, August 20, 1847.

[6] *Ibid.*, August 21, 1846.

[7] *Ibid.*, October 2, 1856.

[8] See *C. A.*, August 20, 1847.

[9] *Ibid.*, August 30, 1869.

[10] *Ibid.*, July 8, 1872.

[11] For the Lancaster, Ohio, meeting, see John F. Grimes, *The Romance of the American Camp Meeting* (Cincinnati, 1922).

[12] James B. Finley, *Sketches of Western Methodism* (Cincinnati, 1855), p. 396.

[13] *C. A.*, August 14, 1856.

[14] *Ibid.*, March 1, 1844.

[15] See "Should Christians Dance?" *C. A.*, April 23, 1847.

[16] *C. A.*, May 13, 1858.

[17] *Ibid.*, July 10, 1871.

[18] *Ibid.*, December 15, 1884.

[19] *C. A.*, May 21, 1891, gives an example of baseball reporting in the German-language press, which runs as follows: "Der Pitcher Mullane liess in der 6 Inning etwas nach und erlaubte den Gegnern fünf Runs zu machen, wodurch das Spiel verloren wurde."

[20] *Minutes of the Ohio Annual Conference of the Methodist Church, 1895*, p. 38.

[21] *C. A.*, December 22, 1853.

[22] *Ibid.*, February 16, 1854.

[23] *Ibid.*, June 16, 1879, July 5, 1875.

[24] *Ibid.*, April 1, 1878.

[25] *Ibid.*, March 4, 1878.

[26] Letter of Nast to his son Albert, July 11, 1877.

[27] Letter of Nast to his son Albert, November 6, 1888.

[28] *C. A.*, May 1, 1856.

[29] Letter of Albert Nast to his father June 30, 1870.

[30] Letter of William Nast to his father, July 13, 1870.

[31] *C. A.*, August 14, 1871.

[32] *Minutes of the Ohio Annual Conference of the Methodist Episcopal Church, 1881* (Cincinnati, 1881), p. 34.

[33] *Minutes, 1884*, p. 31.

[34] For statistics on the spread of German Methodism, and the development of its separate organizations, see the annual reports in the *C. A.*, and also Otto E. Kriege, *Geschichte des Methodismus* (Cincinnati, 1909).

[35] *Methodist General Conference Journal* (1868), pp. 455-56.

[36] I am indebted to Mr. Donald K. Gorrell for some of the data on this proposed merger.

[37] May 3, 1864.

[38] Letter of Albert Nast to his father, March 31, 1868.

[39] *C. A.*, April 20, May 4, 1868.

[40] *Ibid.*, May 4, 1868.

[41] Letter of Nast to his son Albert, May 10, 1877.

[42] Letter to Albert Nast, November 8, 1888.

[43] See Paul F. Douglas, *The Story of German Methodism* (Cincinnati, 1939).

[44] See *Cincinnati Enquirer*, September 15, 1935, for an anniversary article on a century of the German work.

7

[1] James B. Finley, *Sketches of Western Methodism* (Cincinnati, 1855), p. 307.

[2] Quoted in Paul F. Douglas, *The Story of German Methodism* (Cincinnati, 1939), p. 60.

[3] W. C. Barclay, *Early American Methodism, 1769-1844* (2 vols., New York, 1949), I, 274 *et seq.*

[4] Also " wie hart ist es andern gegangen," " recommendirt," etc. See *C. A.*, April 24, 1871.

[5] *C. A.*, April 3, 1871.

⁶ *Ibid.*, June 8, 1868.
⁷ *Ibid.*, November 11, 1872.
⁸ *Ibid.*, September 5, 1881.
⁹ XXXIX (July, 1857), 428-36.
¹⁰ *C. A.*, December 22, 1859.
¹¹ *Ibid.*, October 4, 1844.
¹² *Ibid.*, February 23, 1880.
¹³ *Ibid.*, May 11, 1868.
¹⁴ *Ibid.*, April 19, 1875.
¹⁵ *Ibid.*, January 26, 1888.
¹⁶ *Ibid.*, March 22, 1844.
¹⁷ *Ibid.*, January 19, 1854.
¹⁸ *Ibid.*, January 18, 1864.
¹⁹ *Ibid.*, May 4, 1868.
²⁰ *Ibid.*, October 4, 1880.
²¹ See, e. g., the issues of June 5, 1890 and June 7, 1894.
²² *C. A.*, February 2, 1888.
²³ *Ibid.*, October 26, 1899.
²⁴ *Ibid.*, May 19, 1853.

8

¹ *C. A.*, September 6, 1844.
² *Ibid.*, December 19, 1861.
³ *Ibid.*, December 22, 1859.
⁴ *Ibid.*, December 20, 1844.
⁵ *Ibid.*, March 1, 1855.
⁶ *Ibid.*, May 7, 1857.
⁷ *Ibid.*, January 31 and March 14, 1861.
⁸ *Ibid.*, May 2, 1861.
⁹ *Ibid.*, October 17, 1861.
¹⁰ *Ibid.*, May 2, 1861.
¹¹ *Ibid.*, November 30, 1863.
¹² Nast secured most of his information from a careful scrutiny of his exchanges, which included not only American papers, like the *Cincinnati Volksblatt* and the *Freie Presse*, the New York *Abendzeitung*, the New York *Staatszeitung*, the *St. Louis Westliche Post*, the New York *World*, *Evening Post*, *Tribune*, *Herald* and *Post*, the *Cincinnati Commercial*, the *Louisville Journal*, the *Philadelphia Inquirer*, but also foreign papers, like the *Kölner Zeitung*, *Augsburger Allgemeine Zeitung*, *Karls-*

ruher Zeitung, the London *Herald, Economist, Daily News* and *Times*, and the Paris *Temps*. He also relied heavily on such leading German-language papers as the Baltimore *Wecker*, the *New Yorker Criminal Zeitung*, the New York *Handelszeitung* and, especially, the *Illinois Staats-zeitung*.

[13] See Carl Wittke, *Refugees of Revolution, the German Forty-Eighters in America* (Philadelphia, 1952), Chapter XVI.

[14] *C. A.*, April 23, 1865.

[15] See Ralph E. Morrow, *Northern Methodism and Reconstruction* (East Lansing, 1956).

[16] *C. A.*, August 9, 1875.

[17] *Ibid.*, June 10, 1872.

[18] *Ibid.*, May 13, 1872.

[19] *Ibid.*, May 10, 1875.

[20] *Ibid.*, November 8, 1880.

[21] *Ibid.*, February 5, 1852.

[22] *Ibid.*, August 4, 1879.

[23] *Ibid.*, June 24, 1872, January 5, 1874.

[24] *Ibid.*, July 28, 1887.

[25] *Ibid.*, January 18, 1894.

[26] *Ibid.*, April 13, 1854.

9

[1] See Carl Wittke, *The German-Language Press in America* (Lexington, Kentucky, 1957).

[2] *C. A.*, August 26, 1858.

[3] See Carl Wittke, *Refugees of Revolution, the German Forty-Eighters in America* (Philadelphia, 1952).

[4] *C. A.*, June 4, 1847.

[5] See *The Methodist Quarterly Review*, XXXII (1850), 671-74; XL (1858), 601.

[6] *C. A.*, February 12, 1852.

[7] *Ibid.*, March 2, 1854.

[8] *Ibid.*, July 6, 1854.

[9] *Ibid.*, January 8, 1852.

[10] *Ibid.*, October 9, 1846.

[11] See Carl Wittke, *Against the Current, The Life of Karl Heinzen* (Chicago, 1945), p. 162.

[12] *C. A.*, December 21, 1852.

¹³ *Ibid.*, March-April 1857.

¹⁴ *Ibid.*, February 11, 1858.

¹⁵ *Ibid.*, March 3, 1859.

¹⁶ See, e. g., *C. A.*, June 12, 1871; March 1, 1869; July 17, 1872; June 4, 1891.

¹⁷ *Ibid.*, July 23, 1866.

¹⁸ *Ibid.*, January 16, 1871.

¹⁹ *Ibid.*, February 6, 1871.

²⁰ *Ibid.*, February 23, March 1, 15, 1888.

²¹ See *The Methodist Quarterly Review*, LXXIII (1891), 721-26; LXXVIII (1896), 479, and *Forty-fifth Annual Report of the Missionary Society of the Methodist Episcopal Church* (New York, 1864), pp. 93-95.

²² *C. A.*, April 18, May 23, 1861.

²³ *Ibid.*, Feb. 16, March 22, 1888.

²⁴ *Ibid.*, August 16, 1860.

²⁵ *Ibid.*, July 10, 1876.

²⁶ *Ibid.*, Feb. 19, 1857.

²⁷ *Ibid.*, January 29, 1872.

²⁸ See *C. A.*, May 8, November 6, 1890.

10

¹ *C. A.*, September 9, 1872.

² *Ibid.*, July 8, 1878.

³ *Ibid.*, January 24, 1881.

⁴ *Ibid.*, August 29, 1889.

⁵ *Ibid.*, July 7, 1859.

⁶ *Forty-fifth Annual Report of the Missionary Society of the Methodist Episcopal Church* (New York, 1864), p. 94.

⁷ In 1870, Nast was considered for a position on the faculty of Drew Theological Seminary.

⁸ *C. A.*, May 6, 1858.

⁹ *Ibid.*, June 18, 1857.

¹⁰ See John Baldwin, "History of Berea Community," mss. in the Western Reserve Historical Society Library in Cleveland, and David Lindsey, "A 'Backwoods Utopia': The Berea Community of 1836-37," in *The Ohio Historical Quarterly*, LXV, No. 3 (July, 1956), 272-96.

¹¹ *C. A.*, June 22, 1868.

¹² *Ibid.*, August 24, 1874.

¹³ *Ibid.*, June 11, 1891.

[14] For reports on the Warrenton school, see *ibid.*, July 6, 1868, and June 23, 1879.

[15] For further data, see Paul F. Douglas, *The Story of German Methodism* (Cincinnati, 1939), Chapter X.

[16] *Ibid.*, pp. 181-83.

[17] For reports on the Berea institution, see *C. A.*, July 17, 1865, September 21, 1868.

[18] For more details, see Douglas, *op. cit.*, Chapter IX.

11

[1] " Dr. William Nast on Rationalism," *The Methodist Quarterly Review*, LXXII (1890), 277.

[2] (Cincinnati, 1865), pp. 8-9.

[3] See William Nast, " The Divine Human Person of Christ," in *The Methodist Quarterly Review*, XLII (1860), 443.

[4] *Ibid.*, p. 445.

[5] *C. A.*, January 7, 1884.

[6] *Ibid.*, December 5, 1881.

[7] *Ibid.*, January 28, 1892.

[8] January 22, 1875.

[9] *C. A.*, December 30, 1858.

[10] See, for example, the discussions in the *Apologete* throughout much of 1879.

[11] *C. A.*, March 4, 1878.

[12] Letter of Nast to his son Albert, December 10, 12, 1884.

[13] *C. A.*, January 17, 1856.

[14] For reviews of *Das Leben und Wirken des Johannes Wesley und seine Haupt-Arbeiten bearbeitet nach den besten englischen Quellen* (Cincinnati, 1852), see *The Methodist Quarterly Review*, XXXII (1850), 501; XXXIV (1852), 482.

[15] The copy in the library of Ohio Wesleyan University belonged to Nast's friend, M. J. Cramer, and contains some of his notes.

[16] Nast's catechism begins with the question, " What should be my chief concern? " and the answer follows, " The salvation of my soul," and continues, " for what does it profit a man if he gain the whole world and lose his own soul! "

[17] See a review in *The Methodist Quarterly Review*, XLIII (1861), 165-66. The reviewer found the section on homiletics " slightly irksome."

[18] pp. 323-24.
[19] p. 507.
[20] *The Methodist Quarterly Review*, XLVI (1864), 513-15.
[21] *Ibid.*, L (1868), 30-56.

12

[1] *A New History of Methodism*, edited by W. J. Townsend, H. B. Workman and George Eayrs (2 vols., London, 1909), pp. 399 *et seq.*

[2] See *C. A.*, October 24, 1844; April 25, August 29, 1845.

[3] See Heinrich Mann, *Ludwig S. Jacoby* (Bremen, 1892), pp. 20-22.

[4] *C. A.*, January 26, 1854.

[5] *Ibid.*, August 5, 1852.

[6] *Ibid.*, July 9, 1866.

[7] *Ibid.*, July 8, 1852.

[8] *Ibid.*, April 1, 1852.

[9] *Ibid.*, February 19, 1852.

[10] *Ibid.*, May 28, 1880.

[11] See also *Ibid.*, May 27, 1867.

[12] *Ibid.*, May 14, 1866.

[13] For more details on the progress of the German missions, see Ludwig Jacoby, *Geschichte des Britischen Methodismus* (Bremen, 1870), Part II, pp. 188-248, 277-337, and Paul F. Douglas, *The Story of German Methodism* (Cincinnati, 1939), p. 129 and Chapter VIII.

[14] For the origin of the deaconess movement in Germany, see *The Methodist Quarterly Review*, LXX (1888), 770-771.

[15] Abel Stevens, *History of the Methodist Episcopal Church in the United States of America* (New York, 1867), IV, 483-84.

[16] *C. A.*, July 15, 1858.

[17] See also F. A. Norwood, " Frankfurt-am-Main and Baldwin-Wallace College," *The Ohio State Archaeological and Historical Quarterly*, LX (January, 1951), 26-27.

[18] See *The Methodist Quarterly Review*, XL (1858), 427-41, 538-51.

[19] See e. g., *C. A.*, July 2, 1857.

[20] Letter of Nast to his son Albert, July 4, 1877.

[21] From Reutlingen, August 15, 1877.

13

[1] *C. A.*, May 30, June 6, 1861.
[2] *Ibid.*, August 17, 1868.

14

[1] X (1866), 632-35.
[2] James E. Pollard, *The Journal of Jay Cooke* (Columbus, 1935), p. 26.
[3] *C. A.*, June 17, 1897.
[4] *Ibid.*, May 18, 25, 1899.

INDEX

A

Adams, Henry, 196

Adams, Green, 199-200

Ahrens, Wilhelm, 46, 152

Albrecht, Jakob, 36

Altgeld, John Peter, 118

"America letters," 11

American Agriculturist, 106

American Bible Society, 60

American Federation of Labor, 118

Americanization of immigrants, 79-80, 103-104, 120-21, 131-36, 190-91

Andrews, Josephine Pulte Nast, 197, 216-18

Andrews, William Joseph, 217-18

Anti-Semitism, 101

Anzeiger des Westens, 98

Apologete, Der Christliche, 10, 37, 38, 46, 54, 55, 57, 59, 61, 63, 66, 69, 70, 77, 80, 139, 140, 141, 146, 148, 149, 155, 157, 159, 161, 168, 169, 170, 179, 181, 185, 189, 190, 195, 214, 222, 223, 226; as a religious journal, 86-102; as a news journal 87-88; advertising in, 88, 104-7; circulation of, 85-86; style of, 88-89; on the Mexican War, 108-9; on slavery, 109-11; on the Civil War, 111-15; on the Revolution of 1848, 122-26; foreign news in, 121-130

designed by S. R. Tenenbaum

manuscript edited by Alexander Brede

set in Linotype Fairfield and Goudy Text

printed on Warren's Olde Style Antique Wove paper

bound in Columbia Mills Atlantic linen

manufactured in the United States of America

DATE DUE

GAYLORD			PRINTED IN U.S.A.